MEETINGS

How to Make Them Work for You

MEETINGS
How to Make Them Work for You

JOHN E. TROPMAN

with

GERSH MORNINGSTAR

VNR VAN NOSTRAND REINHOLD COMPANY

Library of Congress Catalog Card Number: 84-7504
ISBN: 0-442-28297-4

Manufactured in the United States of America

Published by Van Nostrand Reinhold Company Inc.
135 West 50th Street
New York, New York 10020

Van Nostrand Reinhold Company Limited
Milly Millars Lane
Wokingham, Berkshire RG11 2PY, England

Van Nostrand Reinhold
480 Latrobe Street
Melbourne, Victoria 3000, Australia

Macmillan of Canada
Division of Gage Publishing Limited
164 Commander Boulevard
Agincourt, Ontario M1S 3C7, Canada

15 14 13 12 11 10 9 8 7 6 5 4 3 2 1

Library of Congress Cataloging in Publication Data

Tropman, John E.
  Meetings, how to make them work for you.

  Bibliography: p.
  Includes index.
    1. Committees—Handbooks, manuals, etc. 2. Meetings—
Handbooks, manuals, etc. I. Morningstar, Gersh.
II. Title.
AS6.T727 1984   658.4'56   84-7504
ISBN 0-442-28297-4

Preface

Meetings. Committees. They bedevil us. They frustrate us. They upset our digestion. And they are absolutely necessary to almost everything we do. They are not only a fact of life; they are an *essential* fact of life.

In our increasingly complex technical-industrial society, whether we like it or not, it is almost impossible for an important decision to be made that does not, in some way, involve groups or consultation with groups. Everything from the laws that govern us to the brands of food available to us in the supermarket, from the features of the automobiles we buy and drive to the medical procedures that save our lives, all are the result of collective decision making at one or more levels.

Decision-making groups have always been essential to the effective and efficient operation of society. As society moves toward ever increasing complexity, as the quantity of information that must be handled continues to pyramid, as the need to allocate limited human and natural resources among competing interests on something approximating an equitable basis grows, and as the task of maintaining social order in an acceptable fashion continues to require ever increasing amounts of financial and physical energy, the role of collective decision making takes on an even greater measure of importance.

There are few businesses or organizations in which the autocratic decision maker can long survive. And, the larger or more complex the group, the less the prospects of survival.

In government of any form, but particularly in a democracy, which is by definition an on-going group process, there is no room for the independent-minded decision maker who functions in a vacuum, heedless of the input of others. Even the most authoritarian and repressive despot can maintain tyrannical control only with the tacit sufferance of those who are dominated. Coups, putsches, revolutions, assassinations, and so on, are mechanisms by which the governed make their dissatisfaction known, by which the autocrat receives feedback on his or her decision making process. These mechanisms have direct analogs in democracies and in organizations.

Indeed, in any organization, be it a business, an institution, or a society, for profit or for altruistic purposes the committees and meetings that group decision making gives rise to are all too frequently viewed as thieves of precious time. Meetings are amost universally detested. They make our teeth itch. After all, is it not true that a camel is a horse designed by a committee?

Let's start there. Let's suppose that it *is* true that the camel is a product of a committee. The implied corollary, then, is that the horse was designed by an individual. We could rest our case on that corollary alone, for the camel in its environment—the desert—is stronger, smarter, more resistant to disease, better adapted, even faster in many terrains, and has far greater stamina than the horse. But we don't have to rest our case there. The evidence is persuasive and overwhelming that, when properly understood and engaged in, decisions that are a product of the group are superior in almost every way to those that are not.

When properly understood and engaged in—there's the rub and the reason for this book. While nearly everyone professes to understand how meetings and the group decision process work, in fact very few people do. At best, meetings tend to be poorly structured, badly managed, haphazardly conducted, and time wasting affairs, where things get done almost by accident and decisions are all too frequently pre-arranged matters. At worst, meetings are exercises in extreme disorganization, frequently bordering on chaos.

A meeting, then, is an instrument of extraordinary power that is all too often used with astonishing ineptitude. This book is designed to bring that power at least under partial control so that the instrument can be employed more appropriately. While those who dedicate their lives to the hatred of committees (and meetings committees breed like shad during the spawning season) may not come to love the process, they may at least come to appreciate it more than they have in the past.

If you do as this little book urges, I will not promise that high quality decisions will automatically follow. Too many other factors are involved, inlcuding the very quality of the minds that engage in the collective thinking process. But I can promise that the decisions your group, company, organization, or institution makes will be better, wiser, more carefully considered, and more satisfying both to the decision makers and to those whom the decisions affect.

This book, then, takes the contentious committee and the miserable meeting and shows you how you can, with a small amount of effort, make them work as they were meant to. I will give you some things to do that can improve both your meetings and the quality of decisions that flow from them. You are not going to have to learn any new technology or even any new complex jargon. What I will show you will not require any fancy new equipment. All the tools you need for significant improvement are in your hands already, as you will discover. What the pages that follow will do is to show you how to use them more effectively.

John E. Tropman
Ann Arbor, Michigan

Acknowledgments

Many people have contributed to the ideas represented in this book. Harold Johnson and Jack Rothman of the University of Michigan provided unfailing perspective, support and comment. Elmer J. Tropman of the Heinz Foundation, Pittsburgh was always ready with a practitioner's perspective. The United Way of Windsor, Ontario, and the professional development staff of the University of Michigan provided occasions in which some of these ideas could be tested. And special thanks go to the hundreds of individuals who, over the course of many years, have participated in the discussions of meetings and committees—the way they should run, the way they could run. It is with deep appreciation to them that this book is offered as a partial reward for their investment.

Contents

PART V. COMMITTEEMANSHIP / 163

PART VI. CONCLUSION / 195

MEETINGS

How to Make Them Work for You

PART I. WHY THINGS
GO WRONG

Imagine yourself sitting in the audience of one of the nation's great symphony orchestras. The program is blank. The lights dim. The conductor emerges from the wings and bows to the applause of the audience. Then he speaks to the audience through a microphone and asks them what they would like to hear. He explains that he did not pick a program because he wanted everyone to have a chance to suggest selections they would enjoy. He did not want to prejudge the evening's entertainment or have a closed system.

Various members of the audience speak up, asking for this and that. Discussion ensues. The orchestra knows certain pieces—does not know others—knows parts of still others—has the music for only some of the requests. With the evening half gone, a consensus program is finally arrived at.

The conductor then has a hurried chat with the wind section and addresses the audience. It seems that two of the pieces to be played have oboe solos in the third movements, and the oboist has another engagement. To accommodate that musician, therefore, the orchestra will play those two third movements first and then complete the remainder of the pieces in order.

Impossible? Perhaps—in music. But in meetings and committee work this scenario is the norm, not the exception. Committees, so the saying goes, are groups that take minutes to waste hours. They are groups of the inept, appointed by the incompetent, to perform the impossible.

In his collection *A Stress Analysis of a Strapless Evening Gown,* Robert A. Baker has included an article by Warren Weaver called "Report of the Special Committee." Weaver's point is that committee activity is so poor, and committee reports are so useless, that prepackaged sets of alternative conclusions should be available. Such conclusions would simplify committee work enormously by allowing the committee to place an "X" beside the proper statement. It is somewhat curious that such groups are uniformly regarded as useless, if harmless.

But maybe not so harmless. Gary Wills's book on the Kennedy years, *The Kennedy Imprisonment,* is rife with references to the dislike by the Kennedy crowd of the Eisenhower "committee" style. Wills quotes Norman Mailer on Kennedy; for Mailer, Kennedy was ending the era of the small town, of the committee:

> The small town mind is rooted—it is rooted in the small town—and when it attempts to direct history, the results are disastrously colorless because the instrument of world power which is used by the small town mind is the committee. Committees do not create, they merely proliferate, and the incredible dullness wreaked upon the American landscape in Eisenhower's eight years has been the triumph of the corporation. (p. 145)

Committees, meetings, are all thought to be a waste of time. Things go wrong there, we think, because they are *meant* to go wrong. Work of any importance does not go on in groups—it goes on when one is alone.

In this matter, as in so many others that occupy our time and energies, what we think has no basis in reality. Meetings and committees foul up because we don't know how to work with them, because we spend no time in preparation, and because we expect failure to occur (and are perversely pleased when it does).

"Meeting meaninglessness" and "committee constipation" are luxuries we can no longer afford. We have no choice but to make committees and meetings more effective and efficient. It *is* possible to do so, and that's what this book is all about.

1

The Committee Curiosity

"If I were chairman of this gang . . ."
—W. S. Gilbert, *The Grand Duke*

A very effective fund-raising consultant to one of America's most prestigious universities has an unusual clause in his consulting contract. His client agrees to pay him double his normal hourly rate for every meeting he is required to attend and triple his hourly rate for every committee he is required to head. He insisted on that clause because he hates committees and has contempt for the committee process. "If I'm going to be forced to waste my time," he says, "I'm going to be well paid for it."

He is not alone. Each of us who has ever toiled in the vineyards of the American workplace has a horror story or two about committees to contribute to the popular lore.

The very idea of a committee seems to strike at the heart of our cherished notions of individualism. Americans are do-it-yourselfers. Americans are self-reliant. The thought of having to endure a committee meeting is repugnant.

The achievement of a goal is a very personal, individual thing. We don't want there to be any doubt in anybody's mind who deserves credit for that achievement. We cheered when Ayn Rand's architect hero blew up his housing complex because its design had been bastardized by a committee. We smile when people say, as they invariably do, that a camel is a horse designed by a committee. We nod in agreement when someone observes that a committee is a thing that keeps minutes and wastes hours. And, in the minds of many, there is the nagging suspicion that committees may be downright un-American. After all, aren't the communist nations ruled by Central Committees?

Well, the good news is that American society thinks it is a collection of individualists. The bad news is that what it thinks is for the most part a myth. For better or for worse, the day-to-day business of living, of learning, of working, of running companies and factories and organizations, of simply being a part of American society, is largely a matter of group activity. We systematically devalue that activity, but the fact is we *need* other people to help us accomplish our social purposes.

IF YOU CAN'T LICK 'EM, JOIN 'EM!

One of the major ways in which this group activity occurs is through committees and meetings. You have already spent a lot of time in meetings, and you're going to be spending a lot more time in the future. You can either continue to do a slow burn over the time you "waste" in such meetings, or, by gaining an understanding of how the meeting process can and should work, you can take advantage of perhaps that most powerful organizational tool available to you.

It is almost astonishing that so many people understand so little about something as powerful as the committee process. In place of that understanding there is a common, broad base of shared ignorance. A man we once knew used to infuriate his wife by calling her "the committee." Everyone knew what he meant: his wife represented power, inappropriately and ineptly used to interfere with his achievement of his goals and purposes. It was a definition everyone could agree upon, and it was a definition that couldn't be further from the truth.

It is a fact of life that we all might just as well get used to: modern society is run by committees whose decisions affect us all. Boards of directors, executive committees, task forces, staff committees—all are involved in the day-to-day running of the business world and our society. The curiosity is that we spend so much time complaining about the number of meetings we have to attend and the number of unproductive hours we waste in committee meetings and conferences.

Just how much time is spent in meetings? Surveys we've done in training sessions suggest that for active managers, more than 50% of their official work week may be spent in meetings and conferences. We say "official" because most of these women and men take work home with them, work that they could have accomplished (they think) on the job if they hadn't been in meetings.

Meetings are expensive, no question about it. The annual meeting cost for a manager making $40,000 a year is $20,000 or more. A single, two-hour meeting of ten people, each making $20 an hour, will cost an organization more than $400 in meeting time alone. And that doesn't include preparation costs, preparation time, and other related expenses. Doesn't it make a certain amount of good sense to want to get some value for the money meetings cost?

The fact is, in this time of tight budgets and retrenchments across the board, a much greater interest has to be taken in all facets of an organization's life. There is no question in anyone's mind that meetings represent one important aspect requiring such attention. Unfortunately, the usual way that people propose to go about doing that is to reduce the number of meetings. Cutting down on meetings is tantamount to a business or an organization's cutting its own throat. It's very likely there *are not enough* meetings being held (of the right kind) to begin with. Reducing the number only serves further to isolate individuals from each other and make the accomplishment of tasks that need collective wisdom more difficult and slower. Thus, in an attempt to save money, we may actually be adding to the cost of the product.

The alternative solution, improving the quality of meetings, was not terribly popular in the past. Partially this was so because ignorance fed on ignorance. Only a relative handful of people understood the power and dynamics of the meeting process; the rest stumbled in the darkness of misunderstanding. As part of that misunderstanding, they concluded that meetings were a necessary evil not really susceptible to improvement.

Fortunately, like most other conclusions drawn from the lack of knowledge, this one is wrong. The quality of meetings can be improved (sometimes dramatically) with relative ease. People with whom we have talked, for example, suggest that about half the items in most meetings do not need to be discussed there, and in fact can be better handled elsewhere. They also suggest that about half the time is not needed. So, it is possible to cut down on items and time, a step that simultaneously improves the quality of decisions.

In a sense, *decisions* more than committees and meetings are what this book is about. We want to help you improve the quality of your decision making. Decisions represent one of the three major resources that the modern organization has to deal with. The others are money and people; but, without a set of decisions to guide them, money and people have no direction and purpose. It's like an orchestra with players and instruments but no score.

Whereas a good deal of attention has been given to managing money and managing people (what responsible business does not have fiscal management and personnel management policies?), relatively little in the way of energy and resources has been directed to the task of improving the quality of decisions within an organization. Such an effort, if it is to be successful, means that committees and meetings must be improved because they are the largest source of organizational decisions.

Decisions, because they're outputs of the decision process, can't be improved very much after they are made. That would be a bit like making an automobile in a sloppy fashion and then trying to fix it up later. The more sensible course, and the one we advocate here, is to improve the process of decision production so that, as each decision rolls off the decision assembly line, we can be sure it is of the highest possible quality.

This point of view puts committees and decisions in a new perspective. We see decisions and their quality as an important organizational component, perhaps *the* most important. We also see committees and meetings as the prime assembly line that invents, shapes, and ultimately produces decisions. The better we can make that assembly line, the better its product will be. We propose assessing the product—the decision—at the end of the process in a systematic way, and using the knowledge gained from that assessment to improve the process next time around.

We fully expect you to be suspicious. Indeed, if your reaction is typical, at this point you're probably saying something like, "Oh, hell, I spend enough time in committees already. Why should I waste even more time reading and learning about such an ineffective social group?"

There are two answers to that question. First, committees and groups as makers of decisions are the wave of the future. In many respects the future's already here. Japanese group participation techniques should have amply illustrated that. So, in a sense, committees have a lot in common with computers. We may sometimes resent them. We may feel awkward around them. We may not really want to engage ourselves with them. We may want to retreat from them. But, we can't really avoid them. The extent to which we try is the extent to which our competitors with more computerized and more committee-ized procedures will outthink us, outbid us, outwork us, and, overall, outperform us.

The second part of the answer is that committees can indeed be improved. The negative public view that most people hold of committees is in part a product of ambivalence and apprehension and in part a product of lack of training, preparation, and knowing what to do. Things can be remedied. You may not believe it now (you will by the time we're through), but committees and meetings can even be a productive part of your day, something that you'll look forward to with anticipation rather than apprehension. We'll begin helping you along the road to that happy time by giving you a bit of an understanding of why things go wrong.

We'll conclude this chapter with the first episode of a pseudo soap opera that we'll call, for lack of a better title, "General Company." Other episodes will follow other chapters. As you will see, it is the continuing saga of Bill, Elaine, Frank, and Sally, and how three of them conspire to bring enlightenment to the fourth and prestige to them all.

"GENERAL COMPANY"

Episode #1: "Sally Writes a Note"

It had been just a little over a month since Bill Kettering took over as chief executive officer of the Omnibus Corporation. His hard-driving, product-oriented leadership had won him his job as CEO. He counted on his openness to new techniques and new areas of improvement within the corporation to keep him in it for a long time.

His time this particular afternoon was spent on going over memos from staff on ways that the corporation could improve itself. Profits were good but not great, at least not from his point of view. The central office staff, he felt, was too large and needed to be trimmed back. He was also concerned about rumors that the central office staff was not as responsive as it should be to requests from the field, and in some cases actually appeared to be blocking some actions. The problem might be related to the company's growing size. It might also be something else that he didn't fully understand. Either way, it created the image, if not the reality, of inaction and buck passing. In addition there had been four or five instances of really bad front office decisions over the past year or so and several other instances of decisions coming too little and too late.

A memo from Sally Franklin, his manager of central office operations, finally worked its way to the top of his pile. He read it with a mixture of amusement and exasperation.

Sally's note stressed her perception that the structure of all kinds of meethings within the central office needed to be looked at very carefully. She argued that a lot of time was being wasted and that the committee structure that was evolving in the front office was a major impediment to productivity and profitability. "We cannot function effectively as a company," she concluded, "unless good decisions come from the network of decision-making groups that exist here."

Bill shook his head. "Of all the things we *don't* need to work on now," he thought, "it's committees—great bunches of people sitting around, talking to their armpits. What we ought to do is just get rid of some of them. We've got more damned committees than a swamp's got mosquitoes. What do we need them for, for crying out loud? Good decisions are made by individuals. I'm the CEO. I make the decisions around here."

At that moment one of the group vice presidents, Elaine Clark, came in.

"You look discouraged, Bill," she said. "What's up?"

He tossed Sally's memo across the desk. "No wonder we've got problems. I ask my staff for ways to make things go better around here, and this is the kind of stuff I get in response."

Elaine picked up the memo and read it carefully. "She's got a point, you know. We all do spend a heck of a lot of time in meetings, and they are pretty bad. Maybe we ought to see what she has in mind. I could get together with her this afternoon for a while."

Bill nodded approval. "O.K., Elaine, but don't waste much time on it. Meetings are a necessary evil, but I don't really think there's much can be done about them. You can define the word "boring" any way you want, but it still means *boring*—or maybe, *committee.*"

2
Why Things Go Wrong

"T'were almost a pity, the pretty committee."
—W. S. Gilbert, *Ruddigore*

We all spend a lot of time in meetings and committee activities. Most of that time seems to be unsatisfactorily spent. We promise you, all that is going to change. The meetings and committees that have tied you in knots of frustration and irritation haven't really been bad. They have just been sick. We're about to make them well. As with any sick patient, the first step toward making things better is an accurate diagnosis. Here are some of the reasons why things go wrong.

A BRIEF SYMPTOMATOLOGY

Group Activity Seems Contrary to Our Values

We've already mentioned that group activity is contrary to those things American's holds dear. Alvin Zander, in his book *Making Groups Effective,* said it best:

> However, readers face a dilemma. . . . [We] are not all that interested in explaining or improving group life. . . . Individuals feel that the organization should help them; it is not the individual's prime job to help the organization. [B]asic values . . . foster the formation of groups that put the good of the individual before the

good of the group. In Japan, in contrast, important values foster interdependence among persons, courtesy, obligation in others, listening, empathy, self-denial, and support of one's group. (p. xi)

Zander's point about Japan highlights a matter we talked about in the first chapter. Somehow, group-oriented values make it possible for Japanese production to achieve goals that may soon be surpassing American quotas. (In some areas they've already done so.) Yes, the Japanese have a somewhat different life-style from ours. Yes, the Japanese view of obligations and responsibilities to employers is somewhat different from ours. No, we would not want to copy the Japanese in every respect. That does not mean that we can't learn something from their experience.

We Americans tend to take the myth of our individualism very seriously. It's especially prominent in our comic book heros: the Lone Ranger, Superman, Batman, Sgt. Preston. All are people working as individuals to right wrongs and achieve justice. But wait, is that really right? Not completely. Ask yourself who helps them, and you will find that each has important assistance. In the case of the Lone Ranger, it's Tonto and the great horse, Silver. Superman's long relationship with Lois Lane has pulled him out of a number of difficult spots. Batman has Robin, the boy wonder, helping him, and Sgt. Preston has his famous dog, King.

These comic book heros also tell us something about the American view of group activities. We want to do it ourselves. Yet we recognize, often grudgingly, that that is not always possible, that assistance is part of the warp and woof of the human condition. We want to receive credit for doing things alone, without having to share it. Too often, as a result, a comic book solution is applied. We have helpers who have been assigned subordinate positions, whom we don't permit to be upwardly mobile into our position. (It is almost inconceivable, given the American treatment of the Indian, that Tonto could become the Lone Ranger if the Lone Ranger ever became disabled or got into a contract dispute with the network. Lois Lane is good in the helpmate role but must remain there. And so it goes.)

Americans actually have a tempered individualism: one that recognizes the need for uniqueness, and at the same time recognizes, but in an ambivalent way, the need for help and assistance. Perhaps the wagon train is, after all, the best metaphor for our society: individual units, bound together for a limited period of time and for limited purposes, which must act in a cooperative spirit if survival is to be assured. However much some might have preferred to take a single wagon across the prairie, it's awfully difficult to pull one wagon into a circle.

It's not necessary for us to change values from individually oriented to collectively oriented, but it is necessary to recognize that the individual orientation represents a problem we must contend with.

Hidden Functions

Meetings and committees fulfill some hidden functions for our society, functions that we may recognize as important but, once again, are ambivalent about. American society has always prided itself on the involvement of those who will be affected by a decision. "No taxation without representation" has become a rallying cry, applicable in a wide range of instances, echoing down through the years. The tyranny of the boss or bureaucratic manager is despised every bit as much as the tyranny of the king.

Some of our values *do* support participation, involvement, discussion, and collaboration; yet these values run counter to those emphasizing individualism and do-it-yourself-ism. For that reason committees and meetings often tend to be shadow affairs in which only superficial discussion is held because everyone believes that decisions have already been made. Bosses make announcements and ask for comments. The members believe the boss has already decided so comments are pointless. The boss says, "I gave them their chance." The members think, "He never gives us a chance." Though each feels that the meeting was a waste of time, each also felt an obligation to have the meeting and to attend it, as if some hidden force were pushing them into an ancient dance. Not only are members made to feel irrelevant and the boss made to feel unappreciated, but the real value of group decision making is not exploited. That's particularly unfortunate because for many of the tough problems organizations face, group decision making can provide higher-quality decisions than those that individuals, themselves, reach—a point we'll consider in a moment.

Problematic Structure

Many of the meetings we attend have a very problematic structure. There are three specific problems we want to stress here.

First, items often come to groups much too late. As a result, the groups must operate under pressure. Under pressure we tend to make lots of mistakes because emotions run high, and, typically, information runs low. It's a very likely time for the kind of thing that Irving Janis calls "groupthink" to occur, a non-process in which other alternatives are not explored because of time and other pressures.

A second problem has to do with the perception of the nature of mistakes that we make. Most of us will agree that we make mistakes. What we're likely to think, however, is that the mistakes are small, trivial ones, errors of no moment. We're not likely, therefore, to look with a critic's eye or an evaluator's discernment on the proposals that have been made. The extent to which they are seriously in error is the extent to which we can wind up sadly mistaken.

The third problem has to do with the individual who proposes the solution to a particular problem facing a group. That individual will doubtlessly review and think about his or her proposal before mentioning it. Because of this psychological involvement, however, the proposer is more likely to look for confirming evidence than disconfirming evidence. Thus, the proposer is the worst one, in most instances, to find problems in the proposal. That difficulty is compounded by the psychological identification that the proposer is likely to develop with respect to her or his solution. Hence, others, who seek to find problems in it in order to prevent the group from making an error, will often find a defensive and possibly pugnacious individual, feistily arguing down the opposition. As this situation develops, it becomes more difficult for the group to modify that proposal. Rather, they feel they must accept it pretty much as it is or reject it totally. If they move to accept it, they may feel like a rubber stamp. If they move toward rejection, they may feel they have to endure the anger of the defeated person.

This tendency for committee decision making to move into affect-laden bipolarity is one that is very difficult to deal with once the situation has arisen. It's relatively simple to deal with beforehand. Some of the rules that we'll be suggesting in the next chapter, particularly the writing rules, will assist in preventing this problem.

Lack of Training

For whatever reason, most of us have had very little training in committee procedure and behavior. Many of our experiences have been limited to a quick scan of Robert's *Rules of Order* and to the actual hands-on activity of committee membership and meeting attendance. It's the rare individual who has had the opportunity to think more systematically about meeting and committee activity and set out on a deliberate course to improve it. Most of the time the negative experiences we've had tend to provide reinforcement for the very behaviors that become problematic.

In addition, very few of us know how to become a chair, how to become a member, how to assist a committee in a staffing capacity. These roles *are* different and require changes in our presentation of self.

To this lack of knowledge about appropriate roles, we can also add a lack of knowledge about appropriate rules. Robert's *Rules of Order* is fairly good if you're running a large meeting. These rules really aren't terribly helpful as guides to preparing and organizing material for most of the smaller get-togethers that are the stuff of our daily meeting activities.

We're also shy on training in ways to pull together information and the people we need to improve the quality of decisions. What we do know about the rules for good decision making we tend to learn on the job on a catch-as-catch-can basis. That's also how we learn what we know about roles. This type of learning may be enough when our meeting activity occupies a small portion of our daily activity. As that activity becomes more important and more central and occupies much more time, however, something more intensive, more formal, more systematic is needed. That's where a book such as this one comes in. It distills the findings of research and the experience of those who have perfected committee and meeting process skills. It then lays them out for you in what we hope is a relatively painless and palatable form. When you finish it, you will know more about the rules, roles, and dynamics than you began with. And that knowledge will lead you and those with whom you work to more effective, higher-quality decision making.

Lack of Preparation

For all the reasons just mentioned, and probably a dozen more, people tend not to prepare well for meetings. Indeed, there's a distressing popular opinion that there is something good about a lack of preparation—that it prohibits people from "premature closure," or that it allows for "free-floating input." In fact, what lack of preparation does is to allow people to have the opportunity to share their ignorance.

Decisions in today's society are complex and require the kind of advance planning that pre-meeting agenda circulation and materials preparation permit. If we don't meet those requirements, we invite the participants to come together on the basis of ignorance, rather than on the basis of knowledge. So much that is important happens when people get together in groups that preparation for a potentially effective meeting must be extensive.

Most of us would agree that the good things in life, the useful and productive things, by and large require preparation. The track meet or the football game requires exercise and pregame workouts. The outstanding orchestra performance requires decisions about what to play, the provision of materials, and then rehearsals. The dinner party requires planning and, often, days of preparation before the guests actually arrive.

It is true that there can be very successful spontaneous events, and spontaneity is an important part of life itself. But don't confuse the occasional and very useful spontaneous get-together with the day-in, day-out requirements of good decision making. Every so often, an individual with no training or practice excels in a sports event. Jim Thorpe is reported to have shot under 90 for eighteen holes of golf the first time he ever held golf clubs in his hands. It is possible now and then for a few musicians to get together and, with very little preparation, play beautifully. And we've all experienced last-minute get-togethers, when friends drop by unexpectedly, and a hastily ordered pizza or mad dash to the grocery store is followed by hours of enjoyment. The fact that these events can, do, and should occur should *not,* however, be taken as evidence that they *always* occur on a systematic basis. Certainly, everyone accepts the *possibility* of spontaneity. It is sheer madness to rely on it for day-in, day-out performance.

It is also possible to **overprepare,** at least for some types of activities. Overpreparation can be a problem for some athletes in some kinds of sporting events. Plays and concerts can be over-rehearsed. Too much attention can be given to some kinds of dinner parties. However, too much preparation never has been, is not now, and never will be a problem for committee activities. Most of us are still struggling with the problem of being even marginally prepared for what is expected of us. In fact, it's casual and shabby underpreparation that leaves most meeting and committee participants wondering what's going on, why they are wasting their time in the meeting, and how soon they may decently get out.

Who is at fault for this lack of preparation? Probably everybody connected with the meeting, both the meeting planners and the meeting participants. A frequent complaint about meeting activities and preparation for them is that no one ever reads the material that is sent out to provide background information for the meeting. The planners say, "There's no use in sending out material because those jokers won't read it anyway." When we interview the "jokers" and ask them about the charge, a fairly typical response goes something like this: "There's just no point in reading the stuff they send out. In the first place, there's too much of it. We couldn't possibly get through it all. Besides, we usually don't discuss it at the meeting anyway. And if we do discuss it, someone is always asked to give a big oral report on it for 'those who haven't read it,' so that it doesn't matter if we read it or not."

The "jokers' " complaints have some justification. Material is often sent out in a form that is almost unreadable. Therefore, most people don't read it. At the meeting itself, because so many haven't read it, it is either set aside, thus angering those who came specifically for it and who did read it, or an oral report is given, validating the position of the nonreader and angering still further those who did invest time in it.

Good preparation, therefore, is essential to good meetings. However, such preparation won't occur unless the investment of time and energy is shown to be worthwhile to the participants and reinforced. Some of the rules we will discuss in this book are aimed at ensuring the integrity of preparation and providing materials for it.

CONCLUSION

Meetings and committees go wrong for a lot of reasons. We've mentioned some of the more important ones here, including those that deal with attitude toward group activity, the muddled sense of decision focus that many groups have, lack of training, and lack of preparation. It wasn't our intention to give an extensive and complete diagnosis but, rather, to provide some sense of the major problematic areas.

The system we will discuss in the next two parts of this book takes off from this point and seeks to regularize and to structure our approach to meetings and committees so that we may take full advantage of the extraordinarily powerful tool that the committee process is.

"GENERAL COMPANY"

Episode #2: "Finding Frank and Getting Ernest"

Late that afternoon, Elaine finally made contact with Sally. While still not totally persuaded that Sally would be able to provide any sort of magic wand to wave over meetings and make them better, Elaine knew that Sally was not a lightweight thinker. She hadn't moved up as quickly in the company as she had without having a fairly good grasp of how organizations work. It was quite possible that Sally might have a few good ideas on how to make *this* organization work better—though it was unlikely that any of them would really have much to do with committees.

"I read your memo to Frank," Elaine said, "and you're right about our decision-making processes needing a bit of repair. But you don't seriously think that the answer lies in making our meetings run smoother, do you? That meeting last year when we approved the purchase of the plastics plant—that was the shortest, smoothest, sweetest meeting I ever saw around here, and the decision was the worst this company ever made. It's also why Bill Kettering is now president of Omnibus."

"But that's what I mean, Elaine," Sally said. "We didn't make that decision. We just rubber-stamped it. We didn't know anything about it, really. Jack Edwards sprung it on us at that meeting, said it was a good thing, and we went along. Sure, it was a disaster; and it got Jack fired. I'm not knocking Bill, but Jack was a very good man; and if we had been doing our job, he'd still be president of this company today. Maybe, if we had had more information about it, if we had had some time to study it as a group, we might have spotted the problems that Jack didn't see on his own."

Elaine smiled: "What you're saying is that two heads are

better than one, right?'' Sally nodded. Elaine continued: "It doesn't happen that way in real life. Everybody has his or her own point of view, and in the meetings we have around here, that means everyone is screaming at everyone else. I was at a finance subcommittee meeting yesterday. It was a ten-minute meeting that took all morning. Nobody had anything prepared. There was a lot of arguing and fighting about our investment policy—and this, by the way, has been going on for the last seven months. We're no further along than we were when we started. Everybody in those meetings behaves like a prima donna.''

Sally began to get excited. "That's the kind of thing that got me to write that memo to Bill. The personnel policy review team that I'm on works the same way. I dread the thought of going to those meetings. I know we aren't going to get anything done, and it's very unpleasant to sit through . . . .''

Elaine cut her off. "And the worst part of it is, those screaming sessions take me away from my real work.''

"Frank's meetings aren't screaming sessions,'' Sally said quietly.

Elaine paused and studied her colleague. "That's different. Get-togethers with Frank Gordon aren't really meetings. Things get done. He makes sure people know what they're doing, and they don't take all day doing it. He knows how to get people to cooperate. But all that's just because he's Frank. He's just got this ability to get things and people organized. Other people couldn't do what he does.'' She thought about what she had just said, then added cautiously, "Could they?''

"Frank says they could,'' Sally said, suddenly realizing she might have an ally. "He's been saying it for years, but no one's paid much attention. Maybe it's time somebody did.''

Elaine stared out the window. Sally couldn't tell whether she was brooding or wrestling with some long-held notion that was proving to be false. Suddenly, her eyes brightened and a broad grin swept across her face. She stood up, walked to Sally's phone, lifted the receiver, and dialed an extension.

"Hi, Frank. This is Elaine. Listen, I'm in Sally's office, and we've been talking about some things that might be of interest to you. Would you have some time to get together with us, maybe even this afternoon? It's something near to your heart. Great! We'll be right over."

PART II. RULES TO MAKE THINGS GO RIGHT

Things go wrong for a lot of reasons. We mentioned a few in the last chapter. Very likely, you can identify a number of experiences of your own that will confirm the idea that committee activity is not well regarded, nor it is terribly productive in most instances.

That's the bad news. The good news is that it is quite possible to make things go better. We're not going to say that application of the rules in this section will transform you into a committee whiz. But, if the experience of people who have used this system is any guide, it will definitely, and very quickly, improve your committee performance, and the performance of the committees on which you serve. People will begin asking you about your techniques and express interest in how you've been able to turn things around.

This system of rules is based on interviews with people whom we would all recognize as committee pros—those individuals who somehow manage to get things done in committees. Over the years the techniques and approaches that they've used have been honed into a sort of set of operating principles that they apply almost unconsciously. We asked them to think systematically about what they do. We took their reports, blended them together, added a dash of research from psychology and social psychology, and came up with a system that works for most people.

Just as the experience portion of the system is a blend of many perspectives, so, too, is the research component. You will not find here a simplistic application of one rule from one particular piece of research. Rather, you will encounter a synthesis of a number of findings from a number of different studies from a number of different professional disciplines.

Finally, we should point out that the rules in this section don't require long hours of training, complex mathematical models, or anything of the kind. Rather, we've sought to present them in the form of straightforward, easily understood principles that people who have had committee experience—and that must include all of our readers—will instantly recognize as immediately applicable in their own lives.

And what is it, after all, that we hope to secure from group activity? The answer is a simple one: *high-quality decisions.* Groups can make decisions of higher quality than individuals. They can spot errors to which individuals may have blind spots. They bring a greater range of perspectives and knowledge to a particular problem. There is also a synergistic effect—the interaction of the group, itself—but the point is to make high-quality decisions. It is to help achieve *that* goal that the techniques we present here are aimed.

3
Some Important Assumptions

"That seems a reasonable proposition"
—W. S. Gilbert, *Trial by Jury*

Before we get into the chapters that detail the specific rules, we need to outline a number of important assumptions. The reason for this discussion is that there are a number of notions, some more preposterous than others, that we feel harm the development of good committee process and high-quality decisions. They need to be corrected before we go any further.

FALSE ASSUMPTION #1: PLEASANT MEETINGS EQUAL GOOD DECISIONS

It should be obvious, now that we've said it, that pleasant meetings don't necessarily result in good decisions; but the point needs to be stressed. The rules we'll be talking about in subsequent chapters do emphasize smooth and well-integrated meeting processes; but we also recognized that conflict and confrontation may, and inevitably will, develop during certain periods. Our goal, therefore, is to make the best and most creative use of the conflict that does develop.

Too often the "pleasant" meeting situation is one in which important differences of view are suppressed, and which, once again, can lead to Irving Janis's groupthink. In this unfortunate situation, the participants all agree publicly while keeping hesitancies and concerns to themselves.

If groupthink represents the problems of pleasantness, then rancor is the other side of the same coin. Most of us have been in those kinds of meetings as well, groups that are characterized by constant conflict and bitter disagreement.

In neither group do things get done. Still, our goal here is not to move from rancor to pleasantness. Rather, it is to achieve some middle ground in which disagreement and conflict can surface and be recognized and dealt with.

FALSE ASSUMPTION #2: THE PERILS OF PERSONALITY

Many authors who analyze committee process specifically and small group process generally, blame bad decisions on the personalities of the participants. Indeed, you often see little characterizations of specific committee and board members. There's Arthur Angry and Tilly Talkalot and Sam Stall, and so on. The difficulties of committee process are seen not as lying within the facts of poor preparation and poor information structuring, but in the particular personalities of the individuals involved.

We don't believe it for a minute. We see the personality as a marginal modifier, not a definitive determiner of what happens in committee and board activity. Furthermore, we believe that the establishment of a set of reasonable rules that provide information to committee members at appropriate junctures in committee life, and the development of understandable roles for committee members, will go a long way toward improving committee meetings, and toward improving the quality of decisions made within the committee context.

This is not to say that personalities don't have an influence. Of course, they do. But we want to stress the point that personality problems should not be seen as the definitive diagnosis of committee problems. Difficulties in structure, lack of information availability, and poor role knowledge are far more likely culprits.

FALSE ASSUMPTION #3: PREPARATION IS INIMICAL TO SPONTANEITY AND PARTICIPATION

Some people seriously argue that if you prepare for meetings, develop agendas, see to it that appropriate reports are sent out to people in advance, and so on, you inhibit spontaneity and create too much structure. Nothing could be further from the truth. That's like arguing that if you have guests over for dinner, you should do no planning, organizing, or preparation because that would inhibit the spontaneity of the guests once they've arrived. Such a dinner party might be characterized by the guests arriving and the host saying something like this: "Well, I'm glad you're here. I haven't done anything yet, so why don't you folks go out into the kitchen, take a look in the refrigerator, see what's there? One of you might want to run down to the liquor store and pick up something to drink. I, myself, am going to shower and will join you in a bit. I'll be anxious to find out what you come up with."

If you think the idea is silly, we agree with you completely. No one would have a dinner party like that. Yet most of our committee meetings are run just about like that. Scary, isn't it?

The kind of preparation we have in mind lays out alternatives and *sets the stage* for committee activity. It in no way preempts that activity. Indeed, we'd argue that without that stage setting, it's impossible to have high-quality discussion. That doesn't mean that it's impossible to have any discussion. The fly in the ointment is that, if no preparation is done, then most committee time is spent sharing ignorance with respect to what might be the problem and what might be the facts pertinent to the problem; that is, what somebody might have found out, should have found out, could have found out that would have brought some level of quality to the discussion. The exchange of ignorance tends *not* to be very helpful when it comes to moving the group toward the solution of problems. Thus, a relatively clear outline of the problem (and alternative definitions of the problem, if appropriate) and some suggestions about courses of action to take are the kinds of preparation we propose.

FALSE ASSUMPTION #4: THE GOOD COMMITTEE MEMBER OR CHAIR IS A ONE-MAN BAND

Our near obsession with supremacy of the individual in American society suggests that committee members and chairs have to play supermember or superchair. If you think about a one-man band, you'll see what we mean. We've all seen such a band: somebody standing up on stage with instruments attached to every part of his body, doing it all. Too many members and chairs act in this way. Often, when you talk to other members of a committee with such a member on it, they complain that "Harry does everything. There's really nothing left for us to do." When you talk to Harry, on the other hand, he'll often say, "The group won't do anything. I have to do it all."

There must surely be a more appropriate middle ground. We prefer the metaphor of the orchestra conductor, whose job is to conduct and not to play instruments. Various individuals are competent on various instruments and must join in at the right time to make the total sound successful and pleasant. There must be preparation in terms of rehearsal and practice, in the selection of the score, and in the preparation of the site. Division of labor and preparation become the hallmarks of the good decision process.

FALSE ASSUMPTION #5: I ALREADY KNOW HOW TO DO THIS STUFF ANYWAY

Many of the people we've talked to concerning the committee process have initially argued that they already know what needs to be done—it is others who are preventing them from exercising their knowledge.

Many of us do know quite a bit about the committee process. Frequently, however, we are unable to assemble what we know in a coherent, operational package that assists us in handling ourselves in the most effective way. The rules presented in this book will not only in some instances add to things you may already know, but will create a framework for codifying much of that knowledge so that what you already know can be put to more intensive and effective use.

FALSE ASSUMPTION #6: WE HAVE
TOO MANY EMERGENCY ITEMS TO PLAN

One of the most common complaints that we hear regarding problems of preparation concerns "emergency items difficulty." People tell us they would certainly plan, they would certainly do an agenda, they would certainly do all of the things we recommend, except that on the day of the meeting or during the meeting emergency items pop up and must be dealt with immediately. Those items can't wait; therefore, preparation is impossible.

This assumption is false for two reasons. First, the more an item is of an "emergency" nature, the more likely information is to be low and affect high. Thus, this is the most difficult condition under which to make high-quality decisions. And, if your experience is like that of most of the individuals we've interviewed, these are the decisions that are most likely to be bad at the time when you most need them to be good.

We recognize that emergencies do crop up now and then. More often than not, however, emergency situations are a result of poor anticipation, lack of proactivity, and poor intelligence about activities going on in the external environment. Part of the preparation process, itself, is a garnering of intelligence about the external environment, anticipating areas of likely difficulty, and preparing for them.

FALSE ASSUMPTION #7: IF IT AIN'T
BROKE, DON'T FIX IT

That phrase has a nice "American" ring to it. It's a real favorite of certain politicians, and one of those quaint homilies that can get you into a mess of trouble if you believe it. Let things go until a problem crops up; then you can deal with the issue. Somehow that sounds so good that it's almost wrong to oppose it—but we do.

Generally speaking, reactivity is always possible, but proactivity is better. You can wait until your tires are so worn out that they start going flat and then replace them. But the trouble that waiting causes and the danger that it may portend is best avoided. The difficulty, of course, is that when things break, you are forced to act and make decisions under extreme pressure, something sensible people want to avoid whenever possible. Rather, a condition of *proactivity,* preventive maintenance, looking ahead, is a much better state of affairs. This requires systematic scheduling and planning, just as you would systematically maintain your car, to prevent problems rather than to repair difficulties.

Prevention also enables us to employ the "leverage principle." The leverage principle says that working modestly ahead of problems (not so far ahead that it becomes foolish) gives you a greater range of options for solution. In emergency situations the range of options is often extremely limited, partly because you may not know what the range of options is, and partly because fixing something that's broken tends to focus effort. Prevention permits us, as with a lever, to use less force (i.e., resources, money, personnel) to achieve desired goals than would be required otherwise.

Japanese organizations have recognized the value of this principle and have elaborate and well-supported schemes for organizational planning. Americans have only recently begun getting into this. For some inexplicable reason, planning and prethinking are still not very well supported in this country.

CONCLUSION

These are not all the false assumptions people make about the committee process. They are in our experience the more common ones. In order to develop a more effective committee process and have better meetings, you need to set aside notions that "meetings are always that way," "committees are groups that take minutes to waste hours," and all of the other negative and hopeless statements that abound. Rather, we ask you to look at committee and meeting activity as a social form that can be improved like all social forms. That does *not* mean that it can be made perfect, flawless, or without peril. It *does* mean that the quality of decisions can be improved by improving the process by which those decisions are made.

"GENERAL COMPANY"

Episode #3: "Frank Gets Down to Business"

Frank Gordon poured coffee for Sally and Elaine from the pot that was perpetually brewing beside his desk. "Bill!" he said as he handed each of the women a steaming cup. "In a way, Bill is a classic case of what Cleaver meant when he said, 'if you're not part of the solution then you're part of the problem,' or something like that."

Sally and Elaine both looked a little puzzled.

Frank noted their confusion, smiled, and elaborated. "Right now, Bill has a fundamentally wrong idea—one very common in business, in government, in organizations of all sort, even in the military—that good meetings are an accident, and good decisions made by committees something akin to a miracle."

"I'm not sure it's really such a wrong idea," Elaine said. "Some of the meetings we hold around this company look more like exercises in jungle warfare than problem-solving or decision-making activities."

"But they don't have to be like that," Frank said. "It's just a case of having a basic understanding of the processes that are involved in group decision-making and then applying a few simple rules to make those processes work as they're supposed to."

"Isn't that just a lot of theory, though, Frank?" Sally asked.

"Sure," Frank said, "but there's nothing wrong with theory that works in practice."

"Well," said Elaine, "I know that something is working in the meetings you hold. We just thought it was a function of your personality."

Frank laughed. "You should have seen me a few years ago. I used to hold the worst meetings you ever saw. I've learned a few things since then. One of the things I've learned, unfortunately, is that it's hard to get people excited about the idea of better meetings. I've tried. I've written memos (to Bill and to Jack Edwards when he was president) till my fingers ached. I'm convinced that as long as Bill thinks meetings are trivial, nothing much is going to change. It'll only be when he begins to see that group decision-making is among the most powerful activities that takes place in any organization that he'll cease to be part of the problem and start to become a key element in the solution."

"I know something has to be done," said Sally. "That's why I wrote my memo to him. But how do we get him to start seeing the light?"

Frank's eyes sparkled, and he whispered, "Conspiracy."

Sally and Elaine looked at one another a bit nervously.

"A gentle conspiracy, to be sure," Frank continued, "but a conspiracy, nevertheless. The three of us are among the top executives of Omnibus. If we work together we can start to change a few things on our own, demonstrating to everyone—and especially to Bill—that things can get better."

"What have we got to lose?" Elaine said.

"Nothing," said Frank, "and that's the beauty of it. I can teach you both very quickly a few tricks of the trade that will streamline the meetings you're involved in and that will help the committees you're on make more effective decisions, more accurately and more quickly."

"If nothing else," said Sally, "it'll make the meetings I go to more interesting."

"It'll mean a bit more work for all of us," said Frank, "and changes aren't going to happen overnight. But if we keep at it, I think you—and everyone else in the company—

will begin to see some dramatic changes over the next month or two.''

Elaine grinned. ''I've never been part of a real conspiracy before. Shouldn't we have a name for our little group?''

''How about M.E.E.T.,'' Sally asked, ''Meeting Evolution and Evaluation Team?''

''That's O.K. with me,'' said Elaine, holding her coffee cup up in salute. ''And we can use the coffeepot as our secret symbol?''

''All right, then, fellow rebels,'' Frank said. ''Now, here's the first thing we'll do . . . .''

4
The Fraction Rules

"You've no right to call me a vulgar fraction."
—W. S. Gilbert, *The Gondoliers*

Let's move now to our first set of rules: the Fraction Rules. These include the Rule of Halves, the Rule of Sixths, the Rule of Three Quarters, and the Rule of Two Thirds. Each of them when applied, and they must be applied together, will help the meeting planner and committee coordinator to have more efficient and effective meetings. The Rule of Halves is a good place to start.

THE RULE OF HALVES

The Rule of Halves says that all candidate items for an upcoming meeting must be in the hands of the agenda scheduler one half of the time between meetings.

RULE OF HALVES
All candidate items for an upcoming meeting must be in the hands of the agenda scheduler one half of the time between meetings.

The first step in planning a meeting is to find out what the purpose of the meeting is and what the things are that people attending the meeting want to have handled. The best ways to do this are to examine previous minutes for items that might be coming up and to ask individuals who might be coming to the meeting what issues and topics they have.

The meeting planner then makes a list of such candidate items and engages in a number of special processes with them. First is the process of item sorting.

Item Sorting

Under item sorting all items are reviewed for relevance to the upcoming meeting. Typically, a substantial proportion (usually 40 to 50%) of candidate items will be set aside as topics for the specific upcoming meeting. The reason for this culling is that most people who are proposing items do not always know what else might be needed to handle a particular item. As a result they may say, "Let's talk about it at the next meeting."

Many of the items are inappropriate for group discussion. They are more appropriate for one-to-one communication, or they may have been handled somewhere else and the individual proposer does not know it. Other organizational factors may determine that they are better handled in other ways. Thus, the meeting planner first goes through all of the items and sorts out those that should not be topics for the upcoming meeting. The individual proposers are then notified by note or phone about what has happened to their item. While their suggestions may not get on the agenda, the proposers do receive feedback about them.

We'd like to stress here that the process of sorting is *not* one that keeps items from being considered. Rather, it focuses on the best way to consider those items. Some do need to be considered in meetings. Others need to be handled on a one-to-one basis, over the phone or in person. The meeting planner has the responsibility for some follow-through so that each item that has been proposed is handled in some way. Only a subset of items, however, is handled by being brought up at the next meeting.

Item Assessment

The meeting planner then assesses the remaining items for informational, decisional, and discussion components. Generally, items are divided into three piles: those that require decision, those that require discussion, and those available for information. This allocation is important because the items will be located at different points on the agenda. At this juncture, however, the meeting planner simply wants to ascertain which of the categories the item falls into. This assessment forces clarification of the purpose in many instances.

So far, so good. We must now handle the delicate matter of committee reports and other kinds of subgroup reports. "The next item on the agenda is the treasurer's report." Right? Wrong! "The next item on the agenda is the report of the building committee." Right? Wrong! In fact, forget about reports entirely as legitimate items for an agenda.

Subcommittee reports, task force reports, treasurer's reports, and so on, must all be assessed for their decisional or discussion elements. Only these elements (and there may be only one), *not* the report itself, should be topics for consideration by the committee. Hence, a topic such as "the treasurer's report" is not a legitimate item. Rather, the specifics of the treasurer's report, having to do with the allocating of specific funds, for example, or discussion about the wisdom of moving in a particular investment direction, become the relevant items.

This means that a subcommittee may appear on an agenda two or three times, if they have two or three separate items. A great deal of mischief, inefficiency, and frustration are caused by the inappropriate blending of topics at one location on the agenda, simply because one committee happens to report them. That's equivalent to letting the violinist play all of the violin parts of a particular piece at one point in time because they are violin parts. Or, saying that a person who has brought a salad and dessert to a party should serve them together because they were brought by the same person. Rather, we need to break up the more complex reports into individual items for individual action.

The old pattern of considering whole subcommittee or task force reports must be set aside. Instead, what the meeting planner does is set up a list of items, some of which are for decision, some of which are for discussion.

Item Analysis

Each item is then analyzed to see if there is enough information available to decide, or to discuss the item properly. Frequently, the meeting planner will have to do some additional work at this point. This may require checking with a particular individual who needs to be present to decide or deal with a particular item. It may involve seeing to it that a particular report is available that is necessary to discuss another type of question, and so on.

A *complete* agenda is not only an appropriate list of items for decision and discussion, but one that also carries with it the assurance that requisite information and people will be present so that the item can be efficiently and effectively dealt with. We'll talk about this more in Chapter 7 when we discuss the Integrity Rules.

Item Disaggregation and Augmentation

Part of the item analysis procedure will suggest to the meeting planner that some items as proposed are simply too large to be handled efficiently and effectively. Too many important subdecisions are contained within a particular larger item. When this happens, the planner engages in a process of item *disaggregation*. The item is broken down into one or more smaller, more palatable items.

Often, item proposers do not sense the complex range of decisions and subdecisions that may be involved in a particular issue. Because of this complexity, it frequently is necessary to break the item down into smaller bits.

The reverse is also true. Sometimes two or three individuals propose variants of a particular item. This calls for a process of *aggregation,* blending together two or three small items that logically fit together, so that a particular topical area can be fruitfully handled.

Item *augmentation* is also necessary. Augmentation occurs when a particular item proposed for discussion or decision requires something more than the proposer realized. Often, for example, a particular decision may require legal advice and legal input. It may be necessary, therefore, for the meeting planner to contact the organization's attorney or legal counsel to have an opinion ready at the time the item comes up for consideration at the meeting.

Here, then, the Rule of Halves is applied: items are submitted to the meeting planner approximately halfway through the meeting period. If it's a monthly meeting, at approximately the two-week point items are sitting on the meeting planner's desk for consideration and review. If it is a weekly meeting, Monday morning perhaps, then Wednesday is a good time to get the items together.

The meeting planner goes through a number of the processes we've described in an attempt to weed out those items that do not need to be considered and to make sure that those that do are appropriately structured.

The planner also does one more thing. He or she places a priority on the items in a particular way. We'll discuss that process in Chapter 6 when we talk about the Agenda Bell.

THE RULE OF SIXTHS

Most of the time the agenda scheduler looks to the current items as the base of the material for an upcoming meeting. Indeed, this accounts for about two thirds of the meeting material. The remaining third is divided into two parts, each constituting about a sixth of what remains.

One of the sixths is material from the past. These items were scheduled to appear at this point months (sometimes years) ago. This material also can include leftover items and other historical material.

The other sixth, and perhaps the more important, deals with future or foward items. Most meetings operate reactively, dealing with those items that have been brought to the members' attention. The leverage principle suggests that working ahead modestly gives meeting participants a greater ability to control their environment or, at least, to explore a range of options more favorable to themselves. Some attempt, therefore, needs to be made to schedule items for future discussion and consideration, from a few months to as much as a year ahead. They should be counted as discussion items. Including these items permits committee members to prepare themselves psychologically for upcoming issues. What may be even more crucial is that such items allow the generation of options for future consideration and more detailed work. The agenda scheduler not only adds items directly from his or her own knowledge of upcoming items, but also asks others directly about pie-in-the-sky type topics that they would like to have discussed.

RULE OF SIXTHS

Approximately one sixth of agenda items will (should) consist of material from the past.
Approximately one sixth of agenda items will (should) consist of future or forward items.

THE RULE OF TWO THIRDS

The Rule of Two Thirds says that all meetings are divided into three parts: a start-up period, a heavy work period, and a decompression period. The start-up period is one in which relatively less-difficult items are handled, during which latecomers are beginning to arrive, and people are "getting on board" for the particular meeting. The middle third of the meeting, the heavy work period, is one in which people's attention is most effectively and most efficiently focused on the items at hand. That's the time when the meeting scheduler should seek to have the most difficult items available for consideration. The last third of the meeting is a decompression phase during which people are beginning to unwind from the meeting activities and in which their attention begins to move, partly at least, toward the next, upcoming activity. It is a bad time for heavy work, and items that do not command the complete and full attention of the member are best put here.

RULE OF TWO THIRDS

All meetings are divided into three parts: a start-up period, a period of heavy work, and a decompression period; instructional, decisional, and discussion items are scheduled to conform to these phases.

The specific ordering of items following this general principle will be discussed under the Rule of the Agenda Bell. However, it's important for the meeting planner, in thinking through the items for discussion now before her or him, to divide them into three piles. The first pile is made up of informational items; the second pile is composed of items available for decision; the third pile should be those items available for discussion. Organizing the items in this way provides a rough outline of the order in which items are to be considered.

THE RULE OF THREE QUARTERS

The Rule of Three Quarters says that at the three-quarter point between meetings, the meeting planner sends out a packet of materials. This will include an agenda, followed by minutes of a previous meeting, if minutes are used, followed by requisite attachments or documents that explain and provide information about items on the agenda.

RULE OF THREE QUARTERS

The meeting planner sends out packs of material pertinent to the next meeting at the three-quarter point between meetings.

Generally speaking, the three-quarter period is adequate for providing people time to review the meeting materials before the meeting. Experience has shown that if the meeting materials get to the attendee much before this, those materials tend to get ignored. If the material is sent out after this point, there is the danger that it may not arrive until after the meeting is over.

CONCLUSION

Some people tell us that "This system is fine for formal meetings, but many of mine are among friends. I don't need to go through all this".

We couldn't disagree more. In fact, it's meetings of people who know each other, who meet regularly and within the same work context, that most frequently go sour. And they use that closeness as their excuse for not preparing. The fact that those attending a meeting know each other well and work together on a daily basis, if anything, should argue for *more* concern and consideration rather than less. Perhaps the best example of this kind of problem can be drawn from the family experiences and relationship experiences that we all have. Despite the fact that we may live in a marital relationship with a husband or wife, that we may have children, that we may have significant others, time and time again we find ourselves surprised at the things those people do and think, things that we never were sensitive to or contemplated. Further, precisely because we *think* we know what we don't know, we tend to ignore people who are close to us and give them less concern and courtesy than we might give to strangers. Though we may argue that we can always remedy that—and perhaps the argument is true—in point of fact we rarely do. Planning and prethinking, therefore, are essential to all decision-making situations, whether they involve people we know and work with on an intimate basis, or involve more casual acquaintances.

The Fraction Rules are a good place to start. The next set of rules, the Writing Rules, help us with the written material that is so important to each meeting.

"GENERAL COMPANY"

Episode #4: "Meeting with Some Success"

By the end of the third week of activity, as the M.E.E.T. conspirators gathered around Frank's coffeepot, Frank was able to issue his first "Well done!"

"Only medium well," Elaine corrected. "We've managed to make some progress, but it's slow going."

"And you were right about it taking more than the usual amount of time," Sally added. "I've volunteered to help set up the agendas for three different committees. That turns out to be a lot of work."

Frank was obviously pleased with the efforts of his co-conspirators. "Agenda scheduling is a lot of work, if it's done right, Sally. But the agenda scheduler is in a very powerful position. That's where the control of a meeting really begins. And things are starting to change a little, aren't they?"

"I have to admit," Elaine said, "we've managed to trim an awful lot of fat out of the few meetings I've been able to work on. We even managed to get something done on the finance committee because, when I set up the agenda, I deliberately left off some of the unnecessary items that had been taking up so much of our time. And, I'll tell you, it's kind of funny to see the looks on people's faces when I get them information for meetings ahead of time."

"A lot of what we do still has a disorganized feel to it," said Sally, "but things are getting better, I'm sure of it. The personnel review team met this morning. We got more done than we usually do and in about one third of the time. This is getting kind of exciting. What do we do next, coach?"

Frank laughed. "So far, you've been following just a few simple guidelines. Now we get to the hard-nosed application of rules. Nothing heavy-handed, mind you, just careful and systematic effort."

"Right," said Elaine. "Our co-workers won't like M.E.E.T. if it's overdone."

5
The Writing Rules

"The insertion of a single word will do it."
—W. S. Gilbert, *Iolanthe*

Written material is an important adjunct of almost all committee activity. It, too, tends to be approached casually and without thought as to structure and form. There are three particular kinds of written material that serve a communication function. One of them, of course, is the agenda. A second is minutes, and a third is reports. A comment about each is needed.

THE AGENDA RULE

The Agenda Rule states that agendas should be written in an inviting and clear way, a way that conveys the essentials of information needed to the people who are coming to the meeting. The use of verbs and the use of the one-sentence summary are important here.

THE AGENDA RULE

Agendas should be written in an inviting and clear way, using active verbs and one-sentence summaries.

Each phrase of the agenda item written on the agenda should be written using an *action* verb. Rather than saying "Minutes," say "Approve the minutes." Rather than saying "The Travel Reimbursement Policy," say "Approve the Travel Reinbursement Policy." It's useful to tell people what is being considered, that is, whether an item is for discussion or for decision. Take a look at the accompanying sample agenda. You'll see how useful action verbs can be.

THE OMNIBUS CORPORATION
Staff Meeting Agenda

Monday, January xx, 19xx		9:30–11:00
1)	Minutes of last meeting (Approve)	9:30– 9:35
2)	Announcements	9:35– 9:45
	a) Office party	
	b) Mailbox keys	
	c) New security photos	
3)	Parking sticker policy (Approve)	9:45– 9:55
	New 18-month stickers are prepared.	
4)	Maintenance contracts (Approve)	9:55–10:10
	An updated plant maintenance contract is up for approval. It is essentially the same as the current one.	
5)	Travel reimbursement policy (Action)	10:10–10:30
	A proposal for mileage reimbursement of $.25 per mile is presented.	
6a)	Proposal for staff retreat (Discussion)	10:30–10:45
	A two-day staff retreat is planned for Maples Mountain Resort.	
6b)	Other items arising	10:45–10:55
7)	"Thank you" to Purchasing Office (Action)	10:55–11:00
	A thank you to the Purchasing Office for the new computer is needed.	

The summary technique involves the inclusion of a one-sentence summary of the item underneath the item itself. Such a summary is not needed, of course, for the minutes; but for such items as the travel reimbursement policy, a statement regarding the essence of the item for decision or discussion should be presented. This gives people who read it a quick preview of what is up for consideration and nails down the specific item that they will be asked to decide or discuss. It serves as an invitation to look farther into the packet to see what the report on the travel reimbursement policy says in depth. Our sample agenda gives you an idea of what such summaries look like. Note how very short those summaries are.

THE MINUTES RULE

The Minutes Rule states that minutes should be written according to three principles: content relevance, agenda relevance, and decision focus. These techniques help to target minutes, remove unnecessary and troublesome verbiage from them—verbiage that tends to be mischief-producing—and enhance their utility as a record of the group, setting the stage for later decision audits and decision autopsies.

THE MINUTES RULE

Minutes should be written so that they are content-relevant, are agenda-relevant, and provide decision focus.

Agenda relevance is a simple technique, requiring only that the agenda be repeated in the minutes, along with its side headings and underlines. This makes it easy for an individual to follow from agenda to minutes to agenda to minutes, without having to search through the minutes for the relevant agenda item.

The content technique says that each item should be reported as a summary of the various points of view expressed, and the decision or next steps listed underneath. All too often people feel that it is imperative to use what we call "process" minutes. Process minutes are of the type that read "he said, she said, he said, she said, etc." Unfortunately, when people find out what they *really* said and how ignorant they appeared in saying it, they often deny having done so. Replies to such denials all too often involve pulling out a tape recorder and proving to the individual that he indeed made a fool of himself.

This kind of interaction only serves to generate hostility and does not help the group to move toward accomplishment. What is needed is not the "he said, she said" type of summary, but rather a cogent and crisp distillation of the main points of the discussion. We use the term "distillation" because the main points are not always made in sequence. That's another problem with the process technique. Sometimes a point made earlier by member *A* connects very well with a point made quite a bit later by member *D,* and an intelligible and intelligent rendition of the item in question requires that those two ideas be expressed together in the minutes, even though they were temporally distant in the meeting itself. For this reason, content minutes are useful. Not only do they make the meeting process more rational, but they also prevent the intrusion of reports of what people said that can prove to be troublesome and difficult.

To provide effective decision focus, at the end of the content summary, the decision or next steps should be underlined or, preferably, typed in a distinctive manner. There are several reasons for this format.

First, of course, it highlights any decision made, even for the minutes skimmer. If there is any disagreement about the decision, or if it has been reported incorrectly, that is probably the most important point to note for correction. The distinctive typing or the underlining technique can highlight that for readers.

Second, it reinforces for readers of the minutes the fact that the group did, indeed, make some decisions. This is a generalized type of reinforcement but an important one nonetheless.

Third, it makes the decisions relatively easy to recall at the end of a year or an assessment period. This recall is crucial because, later on, we will suggest that decision groups should have a decision audit periodically and look at a sample of their decisions for quality, consistency, clarity, and so on. If the decisions are buried in miles of otherwise unintelligible text, the time taken to reclaim them for analysis is too great. Hence, the benefits of decision audits are outweighed by their costs. That problem is a simple one to anticipate and to remedy.

THE OMNIBUS CORPORATION
Minutes of the Staff Meeting, January xx, 19xx

1) The Minutes of the meeting of January x were approved.
2) Announcements:
    2a) The *Office Party* will be held on St. Valentine's Day. Everyone is to wear a costume.
    2b) The mailboxes are being rekeyed. Turn in your keys for new ones next week.
    2c) At the time of the key turn-in, please have a new security photo taken.

3) Parking Sticker Policy.

The new parking sticker policy was discussed in detail. While some were in favor of the 18-month idea, others felt that such a time period was too long. THE NEW 18-MONTH POLICY WAS APPROVED FOR ONE TIME ONLY, PENDING REVIEW OF THE IDEA AFTER IT HAS BEEN WORKING FOR A PERIOD OF SIX MONTHS. Frank Gordon will follow up.

4) Maintenance Contract.

There were no problems with the current maintenance program. THE NEW MAINTENANCE CONTRACT WAS APPROVED.

5) Travel Reimbursement Policy.

There was considerable discussion of the travel reimbursement policy. Several members felt that $.25 per mile was too low in the light of today's cost. Finance members indicated that this was so but that action for change might await a car expense study now being undertaken. THE POLICY WAS APPROVED PENDING NEW INFORMATION FROM THE CAR COST STUDY. Frank Gordon will follow up on study progress.

6a) Staff Retreat.

The need for a staff retreat was discussed. A variety of views were shared, with some feeling that two days were adequate while others argued that three days were really needed. The issue of including families and significant others, as opposed to a "staff-only" model, was also discussed. Finally, there were a variety of suggestions for content. Further discussion will occur next week.

6b) There were no other items.

7) A THANK YOU NOTE TO THE PURCHASING OFFICE WAS APPROVED BY ALL.

THE REPORTS RULE

Reports are among the great banes of our existence. Often, what we send out are very large, dull, and ponderous documents that we know the other committee members are unlikely to go through with any care. Nonetheless, we persist in sending them out if only to protect ourselves from criticism later.

Some people, perhaps, do study them. They are the ones who are likely to be angered by going through an oral rendition of the report at the meeting, a process that renders unnecessary the time and energy they put into preparing themselves, and rewards the lackluster member and laggard who did not make a time and energy investment.

The litany is all too familiar. When we talk to report makers, they complain that no one ever reads the material they send out. When we talk to committee members, they complain that they never get the stuff on time, or that it's too long and complex, or that when they do read it, it either doesn't get discussed at the meeting or is reviewed in depth for the benefit of those who didn't read it.

There is yet another problem, even more serious than those we've already mentioned. The *structure* of reports tends to be such as to invite "rubber stamp-ism" within the committee and meeting process. Rubber stamp-ism dilutes, even eliminates, the ability to consider, combine, reassemble, and integrate that many committees have as their inherent strength. The Reports Rule, involving the techniques of Executive Summaries and Options Memos, tends to overcome these difficulties.

THE REPORTS RULE

Executive summaries and options memos should be the primary sources for effective discussion and sound decision making.

The Executive Summary Technique

The Executive Summary Technique says that all reports should be reduced to one or two pages *maximum*. That is what is sent out to individuals, with the full reports being available for scrutiny on request. In today's tightened resource climate, we no longer can afford to send out volumes of material that we know will not be read. Those volumes are costly to reproduce and to ship (and, we suppose, for the recipient to dispose of later in the circular file). Rather, an Executive Summary that boils down the essence of the report into a couple of pages, with the key points highlighted, will be the kind of thing that individuals can, in fact, look at, study efficiently, and respond to. Where more material is needed or might be desired, the individual member takes the responsibility for securing it.

Information, as we have said repeatedly, is crucial to making good decisions. If meeting planners do not provide this information, or provide it in insufficient quantities, that constitutes a case of information denial. It's equally true that too much information, information overload, causes system breakdown and also constitutes information denial. In our experience, presenting one to two pages of crucial information, with more available, is the best approach.

The Options Memo Technique

The form of this one- or two-page summary is also important. It may be, in fact, one of the most crucial elements in the whole reporting process.

Typically reports follow a one–three pattern: part one states a problem, and part three proposes some action for decision or discussion as to what to do about the problem. Committee members frequently feel a vague sense of discomfort when they receive this kind of report. Something is wrong that they just can't seem to put their finger on. What's wrong is that section two, the options section, has been left out.

We recommend that *all* reports and summaries of reports be structured into three sections. First, of course, is the problem: what it is, its nature, its dimensions. The second section, the options section, sets forth reasonable suggestions about ways to handle the problem. It presents alternatives to the decision-making group. Then, the third section is the recommendations section. There, the committee or individual who prepared the document suggests which of the options from section two seem the most sensible to the preparers, and why.

This system provides the committee with the opportunity to assess the reasonable range of actions that they might take to handle a stated problem. It also provides a way to look at the options rejected by the committee or staffer who prepared the report. Often, this is viewed negatively by the preparers: they've looked into it, why shouldn't their recommendations be accepted? Frequently, they are accepted; but we must remember that it is the committee's responsibility to make the final decision, not simply to ratify decisions made by others.

With the one–three (problem–recommendation) structure that tends to afflict committee reports, committees usually spend an inordinate amount of time discussing part three, the recommendation. During that discussion, invariably, they will seek to elicit the information that has been left out, the alternatives, and to ascertain why those alternatives were rejected. The one–two–three structure short-circuits such needless discussion.

Provided with a range of options and a recommendation, meetings and committees can sometimes arrive at higher-quality decisions than subgroups and individuals can, by combining some aspects of the rejected alternatives with the proposal or recommended choice to improve upon and strengthen the recommendation. The Options Memo Technique, therefore, not only prevents hostility from developing and incipient rubber stampism from occurring, but substantially adds to the quality of the decision.

There is another, professional reason for following this options technique. We are inherently suspicious in our noncommittee life of professionals who say, ''Here's the problem, and here's the solution.'' We may very well have a nagging suspicion that some options have been overlooked, even if we're not sure what those options are. We may also feel that such a problem-solution presentation, even when made by a highly respected professional, even if the solution is obvious or foreordained, somehow deprives us of our right to be involved in the decision-making process. Generally accepted professional practice, therefore, in all professional fields supports the use of this one–two–three technique: one—state the problem; two—state the options; three—recommend one selection among the options, and state the reasons.

CONCLUSION

The Reports Rule comes in two parts: the Executive Summary Technique and the Options Memo Technique. Both are aimed at making more intelligible and more useful the reports that we send out to committees. To the extent that we can achieve that goal, the decisions we make will be of higher quality and more timely, and the process of making them will be less cumbersome and less difficult.

"GENERAL COMPANY"

Episode #5: "M.E.E.T. Buttons Up"

As they finished lunch in the company cafeteria, Sally reached into her purse and produced a small, plain box. She pushed it across the table toward Elaine.

"What's this?" Elaine asked.

"Open it," said Sally. "You'll see."

Elaine opened the top and gave a shriek of delight, then looked about her in embarrassment, realizing that dozens of Omnibus employees had stopped munching and were staring at her.

"You idiot," she said, stifling a laugh. "Where in the world did you get these?"

In the box were several small, white pins, each of which bore the picture of a black coffeepot. "I had them made up at a novelty store," Sally said. "I figured we ought to have a visible symbol of our conspiracy."

"You've certainly got enough of them," Elaine said as she attached one to her blouse. "What do we need so many for?"

Sally put one on her collar. "Well, there's one for each of us three, of course—I already gave Frank his. And I figure as time goes by we're going to have to enlist others into our conspiracy. Each time we do, I'll give them one. Bill will be the last to get one. Do you think he's noticed anything yet?"

"He hasn't made any comment to me, but it's hard to imagine that he hasn't spotted *something*. I told him you and I were continuing to work together. I didn't mention anything about a conspiracy. I also didn't tell him that Frank was directing the palace coup."

"That new system of preparing reports Frank taught us is really working well," Sally said. "There's not nearly as much paper being sent around, and the committees I'm on seem to be taking charge of themselves. They seem to be more aware of options they have, and they're taking a harder look at recommendations people make."

"Same thing's been happening to me," said Elaine. "Hey, I've got to cut out. I'm supposed to be meeting with Bill to go over some budgets. See you later." Elaine cleaned and stacked her tray, then headed off to Bill's office.

Bill greeted her warmly, and they chatted for a few moments about nothing of particular import. But there was something on his mind, and it wasn't budgets. He approached it a bit obliquely.

"How did you think the administrative staff meeting went yesterday?" he asked, almost too casually.

"Pretty well," Elaine said, and then waited for him to go on.

"I thought it was one of the best meetings we've had in a long time. You and Sally were particularly well prepared. It kind of set a standard for the rest of us."

Elaine suppressed a grin. "Well, Sally and I have spent a little time talking about improving our meeting performance."

"It shows. And you know something, something's been happening in several of the meetings I've been to lately."

"Oh?" Elaine asked, with almost too much innocence. "What's that?"

Bill seemed genuinely puzzled. "I really *don't* know. For one thing, we seem to be getting done well ahead of what I'm used to. They seem shorter and crisper, but we seem to be doing more. I'm not sure I fully understand it. Maybe there is something to what Sally said in that memo of hers. I want you to follow up on it even more. Might be a good idea to get Frank Gordon involved if he's got the time. He knows a lot about this meeting stuff."

"Whatever you say, Bill."

"That's a cute pin you're wearing."

"Oh? You mean my coffeepot? It's kind of a club pin. You'll probably be seeing a lot of these around."

Bill looked a little baffled but didn't pursue the matter.

6
The Rule of the Agenda Bell

"Why is everything either at sixes or at sevens?"
—W. S. Gilbert, *H.M.S. Pinafore*

A typical meeting can be a most frustrating experience. All too frequently, we enter a meeting room hoping to begin, only to find that a number of participants are not present. Then the Chair suggests that we "wait a few minutes" until everybody shows up. Another ten or fifteen minutes go by as the latecomers straggle in. Some, who were already there, leave to get coffee. Others may leave in order to conduct "a moment or two of business," delaying the meeting still further. Already the first part of the meeting has been wasted.

All this, of course, is very disrespectful of those who have arrived on time. Unfortunately, it is unconsciously supportive of those who come in late.

At long last, the meeting finally begins, and the first topic is usually minutes. If the Minutes Rule we talked about in the last chapter hasn't been followed, the minutes discussion, approval, and revision can take 15, 20, or even 30 minuts as people review what they have been reading, object to it, seek to have changes made, and so on.

Committee discussion has a way of feeding on itself. For that reason, even when a topic was irrelevant or of very low importance when introduced, once it's before the committee everyone feels compelled to comment on it. A "rule of equity," giving everyone a chance to say something, emerges as if by magic.

But the clock is running. There are no time-outs in committee process. And the difficulties of getting under way, combined with an extensive discussion of minutes, may take as much as the first 40 to 45% of a committee meeting. By this time, there may well be a feeling that effective work is not going forward. People may be expressing some frustration, some disgruntlement, even some anger. The presence of these feelings only compounds the more serious difficulties yet to come.

After the minutes, items begin to be discussed. Since no order is usually found in the listing of items, there's often some disagreement about the actual order in which they should be handled. Whatever the views of the group, there seems to be an almost invariable tendency to keep the most important item until the last. Probably a certain amount of denial and avoidance is operating here. People simply don't want to come to grips with a tough, difficult item. Consequently, other matters are taken up first. Frequently, such false reasons as "Let's wait until everyone gets here" are given. The problem is, by the time the committee gets to the last item, which is the most important one, people are already beginning to leave. Their leaving, in turn, is counter-productive to the effort to have as many committee members present as possible to discuss the last item.

Another delaying tactic that can occur with an unstructured agenda is the unnecessary inflation of trivial items. It's one of those seriocomic situations that occur so often in organizations: individuals sitting around a table, discussing items of consummate triviality, intoning with great seriousness, "This item deserves our fullest attention." Maybe it does, but only for about 30 seconds. It doesn't matter whether such a tactic is conscious and deliberate or unconscious and incompetent. The end result is the same: consideration of more difficult matters, possibly involving conflict and confrontation, is delayed while energy and resources are spent on trivialities. If the difficult items are ultimately faced at all, this usually happens at the very end of the meeting.

Such tactics are bad for the committee as a whole, bad for the committee process, and bad for the individual members. Here's why. The Rule of Two Thirds suggests that the highest degree of psychological energy and attendance occurs during the middle portion of the meeting. Late arrivers have now come in. Early leavers have not as yet slipped out. People are psychically and physically ready to deal with a tough item. (We don't mean that they necessarily *want* to deal with the tough item, any more than one wants to run the four-minute mile. But, given that one *is* going to run the four-minute mile, there are optimum and suboptimum times to undertake that task.) The last third of the meeting is, in terms of group psychology, a period of decompression. People are beginning to think ahead to new tasks and their next obligations. If we run a very crucial issue across people's consciousness at this time, it's going to receive less than full attention. And, because it is in conflict with the member's trajectory of attention (the item demanding attention here while the member's trajectory demands that attention be paid to post-meeting matters), the most important item may be treated with added irritability and pique.

In any event, there will always be some individuals who must leave early. Considering the most important item at the end, therefore, almost guarantees that there will be less than full participation in the discussion. Furthermore, the clock is running. Those of us who have sat through discussions of important items in the waning minutes of a committee meeting can surely recall the desperate sense of urgency that develops. It's the same type of tension we experience watching the last minute of a football game when our team is behind by three points and is on the opponent's 40-yard line. While occasionally spectacular football, like spectacular decisions, can come out of such a situation, no reasonable coach wants to rely on pulling the fat from the fire in the waning minutes of the game time after time. Thus, we need a better game plan for handling committee items, and the Rule of The Agenda Bell helps us.

THE STRUCTURE OF THE AGENDA BELL

Recall that under the Rule of Halves, with its assignment of priority to the items up for consideration, we have items divided into three categories. The first priority is given to informational items; the second, to decisional items, the third, to items for discussion. Priority here does not necessarily mean a hierarchy of importance. Rather, it refers to the order in which these categories are handled in a meeting.

Most of us have had the experience of discussion driving out decision items. It's important, therefore, to locate the decisional items early and handle them directly. We tend to deny and avoid making decisions, and all too frequently our agenda structure conspires to aid us in this process. The Rule of the Agenda Bell seeks to place discussion toward the end of a meeting and decisional items toward the beginning. Informational items come first.

The second type of division that is made is division into three groups of decisional items. Those of modest difficulty are put in one pile; they will become item threes (see Figure 6.1). Those of moderate difficulty are put in a second pile; they will become item fours. And the most difficult item is put into a pile of its own; it will always be an item five. This setting of priorities and ordering is a first step for implementing the Rule of the Agenda

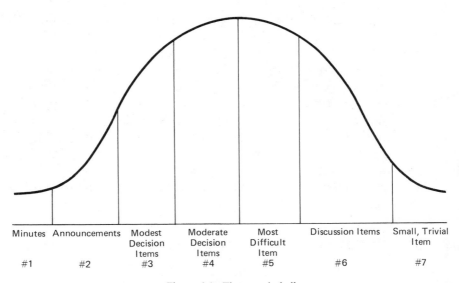

Minutes	Announcements	Modest Decision Items	Moderate Decision Items	Most Difficult Item	Discussion Items	Small, Trivial Item
#1	#2	#3	#4	#5	#6	#7

Figure 6.1. The agenda bell.

Bell. That rule says that items should be considered in ascending order of controversiality to the greatest difficulty; and then, after that, attention should be shifted to items for discussion only.

RULE OF THE AGENDA BELL

Items should be considered in order of ascending controversiality and attention then turned to decompression activities.

The bell-shaped structure of the flow of items across the time available for their consideration comes from the increasing intensity and potential conflict of items such that the most difficult item is always located approximately in the center of the time during which the meeting takes place. After that there is a period of decompression into discussion.

If we were to think in terms of a seven-item agenda over a two-hour meeting, it would be structured like this:

- *Item One: The Minutes.* The mintues, following the orientation toward the writing of minutes we discussed in the last chapter, should be relatively simple and straightforward, each item introduced by an action verb, and the item followed by a one-sentence summary. If there are not enough people available to ratify the minutes officially, then take preliminary action and come back to polish off that detail at the end of the meeting.
- *Item Two: Announcements.* There are always a few announcements. These should be of a noncontroversial nature. It's best not to have a long string of announcements that essentially converts the meeting into an oral newsletter (and the minutes into a written newsletter). If you want to send out a newsletter, do so; but meetings, themselves, should not be used (as much as they are used) for that purpose.
- *Item Three: Decisions.* Item three—and there can be more than one item three (i.e., Item Three A, Item Three B, etc.) —is an item of modest difficulty. This is an item on which

action is needed but which is not judged by the agenda framer to be very controversial.

- *Item Four: Decisions.* There may also be several of these. This is an item of moderate difficulty. The complexity, difficulty, and potential controversiality of the items are increasing. By this time, you should be approximately 40% of the way through the meeting.
- *Item Five: Decision.* Item five is the most difficult item of the lot and should occupy that portion of the bell curve that straddles the middle of the meeting. Normally this would be from about the 50% point to the 66% point. It can be expanded as necessary. There are several purposes achieved by locating the most difficult item in the middle of the meeting. Most of the people who are going to attend the meeting are there. The latecomers have arrived. The early leavers will not have slipped out. The center of the meeting is the high point of psychological and physiological energy. It provides, overall, the best time to grapple with the most difficult item. And, of course, if the item should explode and become even more difficult and controversial, or if a little more time is needed, you can always squeeze the subsequent discussion items to provide that additional time. Once item five is completed, with one minor exception, decisions are completed for the day.
- *Item Six: Discussion.* The item six category includes those items listed for discussion only, and so specified on the agenda itself. Various types of items often show up here. Frequently, those items agenda schedulers think will be quite controversial are first scheduled as an item six before appearing in a subsequent meeting as an item three, four, or five. This tactic can often facilitate the process of decision making, and it provides the group with an opportunity to think through some of the issues before they are faced with making a decision on them. Item six also provides a break. People have worked for about two thirds of the meeting in making decisions. Item five is very controversial by its nature. Therefore, it's just as well not to have another deci-

sion right after that. People need time to shift gears and to decompress. Most of us would agree that revenge is not an unknown motive in human affairs. Thus, the losers on item five might react on the basis of anger and irritation if another decisional item follows hard upon item five. We remove that possibility. Item six is a place where people's rigid attention, which is always riveted by decisional opportunities, can relax a bit. Since we know that in the last third of the meeting people's attention is beginning to move toward matters that lie beyond the meeting, we can be most effective now with less strenuous discussion.

- *Item Seven: Small Decisions.* In order to terminate the meeting and to repair rents in the group's cohesion, we need to engage in a little bit of group rebonding. Item seven serves this purpose. Item seven is usually a decisional item of no great import, one on which there can be universal and fairly quick agreement. The introduction of this item serves to terminate the discussion portion of item six and serves as a one-, two-, or three-minute wrap-up at the end of the meeting. People can then leave and say, "Well, we fought like cats and dogs, but at least we agreed on the last item." A pleasant sense of getting back together again is the last image the people have.

This is the structure of the agenda bell. You can see the logic behind it: at first the group moves slowly, tackling less difficult items; then it moves on to more difficult items, then to the most difficult item; and then it goes through a period of decompression through discussion, finally going to item seven, which is a small item. The purpose of the agenda bell is to seek to combine the complexity and difficulty of the committee's work on the one hand, with the pace and flow of group energy and focus on the other.

Some people ask, "why not take the most difficult item first and get it out of the way?" That may occasionally be a good idea. By and large, our experience demonstrates that it's more useful to have the group begin to operate *as a group* for a while before introducing it to its toughest test. You wouldn't engage in a sporting event or strenuous exercise without a warm-up period. To some extent we're using items three and four as both a warm-up period and a way of getting things done in the process. Also, premature grappling with the most difficult items is apt to leave the late arrivers in a state of pique and confusion. Not infrequently we find that an entire item must be considered again.

Two more techniques need mentioning with respect to item six. Discussion is really a vehicle for opening up perspectives and sharing points of view. Yet, if properly structured, it can also provide useful guides for further action. Structure and organization are needed for discussions, too, because you don't want a rambling, unfocused, and unproductive consideration of ideas. You may, therefore, want to consider from time to time using the In-Principle Technique and the Straw Vote Technique. Let's explore each one.

The In-Principle Technique

The In-Principle Technique for discussion items tries to separate the essential elements of a proposal from those aspects more concerned with implementation and details. For example, if committee members are considering a budget, they may want to look only at the main allocation categories in the initial discussion, leaving examination of the details within each category for a later meeting.

Part of the puropose for the In-Principle Technique is to focus the group on the central items before it and to avoid what might be called "conceptual oscillation." Conceptual oscillation is a moving back and forth between small items of relatively trivial importance and items of the largest moment. When it happens in a meeting, a process of trivialization of primacy takes place in which those items of primary importance tend to be trivialized when linked with items of relative unimportance. Discussion is facilitated, therefore, if the types of items discussed are generally kept on the same plane.

The Straw Vote Technique

A second technique for discussion items is the Straw Vote Technique. This technique is one for placing priorities on the work of staff so that their efforts can be spent in areas of most use to the committee. Consider, for example, an item for discussion in which three or four alternatives of a reasonable nature have surfaced. At this point the members are likely to turn to staff members, and say, "Well, let's get all the information we need about these." And herein lies the problem. Staff time is expensive. There may be three or four alternatives available, but it usually turns out that only two at most are of prime interest to the committee. The Straw Vote Technique asks the committee to rank the alternatives according to their preference. Usually, following such a ranking, the staff members can develop more detailed information on alternatives one and two, and see if that is satisfactory at a subsequent meeting. If not, they can then proceed to alternatives three and four. Often, the essence of a solution will be found in alternative one or two, thus preventing the unfortunate misallocation of staff time to alternatives that, although they did surface as possibilities at the meeting, were not really of interest to the committee.

CONCLUSION

The Rule of the Agenda Bell is a strategy for ordering meeting items to keep pace with the psychological and physiological energies of the group. In essence, items are arranged in ascending and then descending order of controversiality so that increasing committee intensity and energy can be focused on the most difficult points. Opportunity is then provided for decompression and release. Also, the items need to be built up or broken down, shaped, and sculpted to that each item is an entity unto itself and is of a size that people can deal with. Reports (such as the treasurer's report) do not become items in themselves. Specific parts of such reports become items, according to their informational, decisional, or discussion character. As with an orchestra or a dinner party, there are reasons why items appear in a given order.

"GENERAL COMPANY"

Episode No. 6: "The Elite M.E.E.T. to Eat"

"One thing is for certain," Frank told his two co-conspirators as they met for yet another meeting in his office. "Just as soon as we have our project whipped into shape, I'm going to treat you two to the best dinner in town. It's the least I can do for all the work you've put into this. Does either of you have any successes to report?"

"A big one," Sally said, "Keith MacEwen, Manager of Plant Maintenance."

"You mean when he brought in those ten plant managers for the quarterly meeting?" Elaine asked. "I heard about that."

"*I* didn't," Frank said. "Fill me in."

"Well, Keith had this day-long meeting scheduled, and he got so many complaints about the last one that I guess he was a little gun-shy. Anyway, he snuck into my office and in whispers asked me if I could help him. I guess he liked the way I ran that last staff meeting—thanks to you two. First thing I did was make him join the club."

"Did he sign the articles of conspiracy?" Frank asked.

"No," Sally said, "but he bought me a doughnut, and he promised to wear his coffeepot pin every day for the next month."

"Our first convert," said Elaine. "Before long we'll have an army."

"So what did you tell him?" Frank asked.

"There wasn't much time, really, so I showed him how to set up his agenda, dividing the material into informational, decisional, and discussion parts. I can't believe how well that works. In the old days we would start meetings with free-floating discussions, and everything would go to pot."

"I know," said Frank, "and it's still a problem around here. People think that discussion is good—and it is—but too often they use discussion as a way of avoiding tough issues. That's especially true if they don't know much about the issue they're talking about."

"Anyway," said Sally, "Keith held the meeting yesterday. He came in this morning and said it went spectacularly well. Gang, we've got us a true believer."

"I had an interesting afternoon, myself, yesterday," Elaine said. "Met with Bill. He's started to notice things. Told me I should get together more with you, Sally. He even said you and I should see if we can't get Frank involved. How about it, Frank? Want to get involved?"

"He made the same suggestion to me when I drove him out to the airport last week," Frank said.

"And you, of course, told him you just couldn't do it," said Elaine.

"Not quite. I told him I would check in with you two *if* I could find the time. Anybody want more coffee?"

7

The Integrity Rules

"For such is my sense of duty"
—W. S. Gilbert, *Pirates of Penzance*

There are two integrity rules that deserve our attention: the Rule of Agenda Integrity and the Rule of Temporal Integrity. These, like the others, are not difficult. Yet, when they are violated, they can derail a committee as quickly as a few feet of soft ground in a track bed can derail a freight train. Problems need not be great to have consequences.

THE RULE OF AGENDA INTEGRITY

All too often, when we interview disgusted and disillusioned committee members, a scenario something like this emerges: The committee Chair complains bitterly because the committee members never read the material that is sent; the members complain that there's no reason to read it because they never discuss it. This kind of mutual faultfinding goes on ad nauseum.

The writing rules have, we hope, provided enough information about how to structure written materials to maximum effect, that we need not concern ourselves with that problem now. Even properly structured materials, however, won't be considered unless the Rule of Agenda Integrity is followed. That rule says that all items on the agenda should be discussed; items not on the agenda should not be discussed. This rule means "no new

64

business." Now that's going to shake up some of the older debenture holders; so we had better say a word or two more about the reason and purpose behind it.

RULE OF AGENDA INTEGRITY

All Items on the agenda should be discussed. Items not on the agenda should not be discussed.

If we step back for a moment and think, it becomes quite clear to us that, as committee members, we don't like to prepare ourselves in advance, by reading reports and studying documents, only to find that our effort was wasted and other things were considered. When that happens, the committee is giving us a message: "Don't waste your time, dummy!" It only takes one or two episodes of such activity before that message is firmly implanted. Hence, committee chairs and members need to assure the integrity of the agenda.

The agenda represents in effect a contract with the committee members. People need to have assurance that the time they have invested in preparation is well spent. If that assurance is present, the amount of preparation people do will rise rapidly.

But what about "no new business"? Why take that position? There are several reasons. First, new business tends to be that kind of business for which no preparation has been done. It is, therefore, mischievous and troublesome stuff that can insinuate itself into the committee process and then blow up like a balloon, throwing all the other items off course. Precisely because there is no good information on it, committee time is spent trying to find information. Thus, individual A asks about one thing, and individual B asks about another, and the clock is running very fast.

When committee members don't have information on items, they tend to introduce their own misinformation. We know of a man who once attended a meeting in Michigan on the Ohio border. One member came in all excited about an announcement he had just heard on the radio, concerning a budget action the governor was going to take that would profoundly affect the proceedings of the meeting. The group was thrown into disarray, and an hour was spent discussing what this might mean and how the governor's budget action as reported by this individual would affect the committee's work. Finally, it was learned after some hard questioning that the man had actually been listening to a Toledo radio station. The action he had heard about, which had occupied so much of the committee's time, was something being proposed by the *Ohio,* not the Michigan governor.

This example may be a bit extreme, but it illustrates an important point: new business should be introduced via the Rule of Halves, not at the meeting itself. Some will argue strongly, of course, that we must allow for some new business; it's a matter of courtesy and respect. Our reply is, don't do it! But, if you must, at least during the transition from your present meeting style to the more effective approach we are recommending, then put it after item six. Then use new business *only* as an agenda-item-generating vehicle, not as something specifically to discuss at that meeting.

There are other reasons why new business should be avoided. Because it has an almost overpowering tendency to drive out previously scheduled items, it is a serious threat to agenda integrity. How many times have we been involved in situations in which we have come prepared to discuss items, A, B, and C, but, because some new item has come up, we haven't been able to discuss any of the things that concerned us? Not only does new business threaten the integrity of the agenda, then; it also may be a direct assault on the integrity of our commitment to meeting preparation. When other items drive out the items for which we have prepared, we feel let down, disappointed, and cheated.

Still another important reason has to do with who is at the meeting in the first place. Since the agenda is a kind of contract with people, we make attendance decisions based on what we think is going to happen. Those of us who can, may organize our meeting attendance based on a hierarchy of our own interests. As a result, we may come to meetings in part to discuss one or more of the specific items on the agenda. If those items are not discussed, we may feel doubly disappointed. On the other hand, we may choose not to go to certain meetings because the agenda items are of lesser importance to us. If we then find that unknown items cropped up that might have interested us, we will also feel let down. Therefore, agenda integrity is required to keep faith with committee members. Once the Rule of Agenda Integrity is enforced, you will find, not surprisingly, that attendance goes up because people are relatively confident of what is going to happen.

THE RULE OF TEMPORAL INTEGRITY

Temporal integrity is a rule that is both easy and difficult to follow. It has three parts: begin on time, end on time, and follow a rough time order inside the meeting itself.

RULE OF TEMPORAL INTEGRITY

Begin on time. End on time. Follow a rough time order inside the meeting itself.

The management of time is, perhaps, the most violated of all committee rules and one of the most difficult committee problems. While we would all agree in principle that effective time management is easy, should be a natural part of all meetings, and is noncontroversial, all of us nevertheless contribute to its violation.

Ending on time is the most important part of the Rule of Temporal Integrity. Part of the reason for this is that we have other obligations that are temporally linked. Going over in one area may make us late for the entire day. Therefore, committee meetings should always end on time *regardless of when they start*. We have deliberately emphasized this to stress the point that there's an unwritten norm about committee meetings that goes something like this: if we're scheduled for two hours and we start 15 minutes late, we are somehow entitled to meet 15 minutes longer. This is absolute and utter nonsense, but almost everyone shares this idea. And, because it is so ingrained and so hard to overcome, one certain way to lick it is to *start* all meetings on time.

We all recognize, too, that the longer we wait for people to come to meetings, the more we're giving them the message that it's not important to come at the time stated—perhaps not even important to come at all. Thus, what we may think of as a courtesy in not starting until latecomers have arrived, is actually a message that they *weren't* late after all because the meeting hadn't started yet when they got there!

Such ideas die hard. Nonetheless, we need to make a special effort to begin on time, both because the items scheduled require approximately the amount of time we've allotted and because starting on time serves as a powerful aid to ending on time.

Finally, it's important to follow a rough time order within the meeting itself. To this end it is very useful to put approximate times beside the items on the agenda, possibly in the left-hand margin. That will help give people an idea of about how long discussion ought to be. It will also help the Chair move the group to points of agreement as the allotted time approaches its limit.

One particularly effective technique for efficiently handling available meeting time is to place suggested time allotments for each of the agenda items on the agenda itself. If you'll glance back at the sample agenda we presented for you in Chapter 5, you'll see an example of this. The Agenda Bell is based upon the assumption that a only a certain amount of time is available for meetings, and that time should be optimally allocated among the items to be discussed and decided.

CONCLUSION

The integrity rules, then, are simply vehicles that argue for and protect the investment a committee member makes in preparing for and coming to the meeting. Time is one of our most precious resources. Indeed, it is time that committees are blamed for wasting. But committees are not abstract, peopleless entities. They are made up of *us*. If we have a set of reasonable rules for which we can share enforcement responsibility, then a working environment in which meetings are looked forward to with anticipation rather than aversion is not only likely but probable.

"GENERAL COMPANY"

Episode #7: "Frank Finesses Bill's Bafflement"

"Have you noticed anything peculiar going on around here?" Bill asked Frank as they worked on the agenda for the upcoming annual meeting of the Omnibus Corporation.

"No more than usual," Frank said, "what do you mean?"

"Well," Bill said, "there seems to be an emerging obsession with coffee. More and more I see people wearing these little white pins with black coffeepots on them. And when I ask about them, all they do is smile. And there's another thing."

"What's that?"

"I was at a meeting yesterday, and somebody wanted to bring something up that had just happened a few minutes before we met. Sally was running the meeting; and, very diplomatically, she made it clear that we'd deal with the items on the agenda first. Then, if there was time at the end of the meeting, we could discuss what happened. It was a brilliant maneuver."

"Why do you say that?" Frank asked.

"Because the thing that had happened dealt with a tough financial situation; and, if we had gotten into it at the start of the meeting, everybody would have had to put their two cents' worth in. We wouldn't have got anything else done, and besides that, it had just happened so nobody really knew anything about it."

"So the meeting went pretty well, I suppose," Frank said.

"It sure did. And she did something else, too."

"What was that?"

"Well, we finally did get around to talking about what had happened, after we'd accomplished everything else, of course. People made comments and some suggestions, and it was very relaxed. The tension seemed to have dissipated a great deal. Then, right out of a clear blue sky Sally said, 'This meeting was scheduled to end at 10:30, and it's about that now, so I'll entertain a motion to adjourn.' I've never seen that happen in one of our meetings before.''

"Doesn't it make sense to you?" Frank asked.

"Of course it does," said Bill, "but that fact that somebody actually *did* it, and that the group *agreed* to it, was mind-boggling. I got a whole extra hour and a half free because I was planning on spending the entire morning at that damned meeting. And we not only got good things done, but I had time to get to some other work, besides. I think maybe we ought to do the same thing for the annual meeting."

"I agree," said Frank. He unrolled his shirt sleeves, buttoned the cuffs, and reached for his suit coat, draped across the back of his chair. "Now, if you'll excuse me, Bill, I've got a letter I promised to get out to Mike Hayden at the Peoria office." He noticed that Bill was observing him with a peculiar look on his face. "Anything wrong, Bill?"

Bill became a bit flustered. "Oh, nothing, Frank, nothing. It's just that I noticed *you're* wearing one of those silly coffeepot pins on your lapel. Will you tell me what that damned thing is all about?"

Frank only looked at Bill and smiled.

8

The Decision Audit/Decision Autopsy

"At Dover daily he'd prepare to hew and hack behind, before . . ."
—W. S. Gilbert, *Thomas Winterbottom Hance*

One of the most important things groups need to do is to examine the decisions they have made and try to assess them in terms of quality. It's not easy, but it must be done if you are really interested in improving the quality of decisions. There's no reason why decisions should be free from quality control any more than any other kinds of organizational products. And, if decisions are indeed the product of group activity, then some kind of assessment is appropriate.

It's not completely clear in all minds what such an assessment should consist of. We have a gut-level feeling, of course. Informally, we talk with each other about good decisions and bad decisions. After a particularly difficult committee meeting, for example, people may gather over coffee and say something like, "Well, that was a really good decision, and I'm pleased we made it," or, maybe, "Boy! That has got to be the dumbest thing we ever did!"

Unfortunately, gut-level feelings aren't really very helpful. Trying to find out what people really mean when they talk about good and bad decisions turns out to be a very complex task. Nevertheless, our informants have provided us with information that sheds a little light on the matter, and helps establish a rudimentary guideline to use in performing Decision Audits.

Within the framework of the Decision Audit, however, is the Decision Autopsy. Decision Audits refer to an analysis of the regular pattern of making decisions and an assessment of the quality of those decisions. Decision Autopsy refers to the need to take a special look at the "bad" and "good" decisions uncovered by the Decision Audit. Not only do we need to look at all decisions, but we need to look with special care at the best and worst decisions that come out of the committee process. This helps us both to avoid the difficulties that emerge upon analysis of the bad decisions and to repeat the positive behaviors that emerge after scrutiny of the very best ones.

THE DECISION AUDIT

The Decisison Audit is a systematic assessment of the decision-making quality within a particular committee. As you'll recall from the Minutes Rule, minutes are structured with the underlying decision or action statement beneath each item. This structure is designed to facilitate the Decision Audit.

It's important to say right from the start that a lack of consensus—or even an adequate supply of good ideas—about how one goes about a Decision Audit leaves the field wide open. From our point of view, what is most important is *systematic* assessment. And, although we'll give you a method to use if you like, any method that your particular group comes up with would serve equally well, at least at this point in the development of Decision Audits. It may be just as important to apply systematic assessment to decisions as it is to select any particular method.

The purpose of a Decision Audit, like any other audit, is to find out what's good, what's bad, and where strengths and weaknesses lie. As we talked with individuals about how they assess decisions retrospectively, decisions tended to fall into four general groups: those that were excellent, those that were good, those that were poor, and those that were failures. If you think about those four possible outcomes, one fact is immediately apparent: we are not in a zero-sum game situation. You'll recall that a zero-sum game is one in which you win and I lose, or vice versa. When it comes to decision making, it's quite possible for both of us to win or both of us to lose, or for one or the other of us to win or lose to varying degrees. One of the most important outcomes of the Decision Audit system may be the idea that there are multiple winners and multiple losers. We strive for the All Win condition, seek to avoid the All Lose condition, and between those two parameters try to maximize the good decisions and minimize the poor ones.

This kind of assessment lends itself nicely to a grading scheme: A for excellent, B for good, C for poor, and D for failure. The question is, how can we develop criteria or guidelines for judgment that will help us to give the A, B, C, and D designations to particular decisions?

Again, our informants helped us out. Although no one was very clear about exactly how decisions were graded, the rough criteria for grading were implicit in the way they talked about the decisions. The All Win decision was an A decision. Such a decision was one that in retrospect seemed to contain elements in which or from which everyone and everything gained, including the system as a whole.

A couple of points are worth stressing here. First, it's important to indicate that the analysis must be retrospective in nature; that is, a period of time must have passed before an assessment is made. It's very difficult to assess decisions shortly after they're made because we frequently don't know whether they're going to be good or bad until they've had a chance to work. Second, it is *not* imperative that all parties gain equally, only that all wind up on the plus side of the ledger. Hence, in the All Win condition, two of us may gain, but you may gain more than I. That still represents an All Win situation. It's difficult to imagine a decision that results in everyone's being ahead to some extent *not* qualifying as an excellent decision.

The good decision is one in which some people gain, some lose, but on balance more gain than lose. For example, a decision by one company to merge with another may result in some people losing jobs, some reorganization occurring, some product lines being discontinued. If on balance, however, assessment makes it clear that the positives outweigh the negatives, then the decision would be a good one and rate a B grade.

The C decision is one in which there are more losers than winners and/or the post-decisional condition is the same as or worse than it was before. Decisions are meant to improve things, not simply rearrange them; that is, rearrangement must also constitute improvement, or it doesn't get any points. These kinds of rearrangement-without-improvement decisions are called "political decisions" or "get mines" decisions. The focus of the decisional matrix is exclusively on the individual gains of the parties involved. There's no sense of overall gain, nor is there any sense of modifying or tempering one's requests in order to improve the overall quality of a condition or situation.

The D decision, also known as the "nuclear war" decision, is the All Lose decision. It's the decision that, in retrospect, should not have been made. Everyone is worse off for its having been made than anyone would have been if no decision had been made at all. As the reference to nuclear war implies, the results of such a decision can, in the worst case, be devastating.

Here's one way to go about actually making the assessment. Select three members from your ongoing group. Provide them with a sheet upon which are listed decisions taken from the minutes over the past nine months or so. It's important to leave about a three- to six-month gap so that the group of three is not analyzing decisions made recently. You might, for example, at the end of 1985 take those decisions made in 1984 and the first half of 1985, leaving aside those made between July and December of 1985 as being too recent to be evaluated. Each individual reads over each decision and gives it a grade, based roughly on the criteria we've just discussed. Then, an average is calculated.

Two points should be made here. First, three is a good number to use because more than one individual needs to rate the decision. Second, the fact that different individuals are rating and judging will create in some instances inter-rater reliability problems (i.e., the raters will give the decision quite different scores), and we'll look at those situations with particular interest. The goal, of course, is to check your decisional average and your overall average. Look and see, more or less, how the decision group is scoring in terms of these ratings. This information is fed back to the committee and discussed at an assessment meeting. If you observe too many decisions in the C and D categories, obviously work needs to be done to get to the B level. If you have some in B, a few in A, and not too many in C, then you will want to continue the established pattern of decision making. In that case, you'll want to look to the improvement of particular problems rather than to overall improvement.

In particular, however, two things should happen next. First, special focus should be placed on those items over which there is a high degree of inter-rater disagreement. If, for example, some decisions were given an A by one rater and a D by another, then they deserve special attention as they will often represent areas of *goal disagreement* within the committee process. They need to be discussed and followed up. The second type of special attention required is the Decision Autopsy.

THE DECISION AUTOPSY

Basically the Decision Autopsy is a special focus on those decisions that received a D or an A. You should pick one or two of the very worst decisions and one or two of the very best decisions, and look at them in great detail. Obviously, you will want to find out what went wrong or what went right by taking the decisions apart, both literally and figuratively. Upon examination, flaws will be revealed in the bad decisions, and these flaws can be corrected. The purpose of analyzing good decisions, to find out what went right, has the inverse objective of finding out what went wrong. In analyzing the A decision, it is possible to identify the positives and repeat them.

There is another psychological reason for including the A's with the D's. Human nature being what it is, we tend not to like bad news. Therefore, as important as we know it is to deal with the D's, we'll avoid it in the same way we do our best to avoid bad news. The A's not only provide substantive information about what went right, but they also provide an important psychological boost that makes it easier to deal with the bad news.

Decision Autopsies will reveal problematic processes and other kinds of difficulties that stimulate low-quality decisions. The reasons in each instance are usually unique—but not always. There are some common problems that have cropped up in a number of such autopsies. Here are the most typical.

First, of course, is *pressure*. Decisions made under pressure tend to be those rated retrospectively of low quality. This should come as no surprise. Emergency conditions are affect-laden. Information is often scanty. Processing time is often minimal. It's useful to say this, however, because, although everyone "knows" it is true, few bother to "do" anything about it.

A second problem is issue *stereotyping*. Frequently, this kind of difficulty is associated with failure to use the Options Technique or some analog of it. A problem is brought up. Everyone believes it to be the "common problem," the "same old problem," the "problem that we know exactly what to do about." Traditional and routine solutions are proposed and agreed upon. Nobody wants to challenge or to be put in the position of challenging the "conventional wisdom." It fails miserably, and that failure is followed by a round of blame casting and fault-finding.

The real difficulty lies in the decisional process itself. Insufficient options are generated, and there is a lack of honesty about "what everybody knows." For this reason the Devil's Advocate Technique is sometimes useful. Assign one individual in the group the task of raising questions about the recommendation. Because it is an assigned task and one that rotates in due course to every member of the group, no one either overuses the role or feels particularly embarrassed about it.

CONCLUSION

These few observations from Decision Autopsies serve to indicate the types of problems that characterize bad decisions. There are, of course, dozens, hundreds, even thousands of specific reasons that could be added to this list. The specific problems are far less important, however, than the need to sensitize individuals and committee members to the kinds of processes that result in bad decisions and the need to assess those decisions. As we said in the beginning of this chapter, the assessment process, the thoughtful review of a set of decisions, and the application of some set of consistent criteria for excellence, goodness, fairness, or poorness will yield impressive results.

The committee process is now alone among organizational activities in being virtually immune to scrutiny. It is a place where bad work and bad behavior can be almost sequestered. Never observed. Never commented upon. Never challenged. This unique situation stems in part from the fact that our value system, itself, does not support group behavior and in many ways is actually antithetical to it. Nonetheless, we can no longer enjoy the luxury of ignoring the quality of committee work. Change is demanded. Part of that change process will come in assessing the decisions themselves.

"GENERAL COMPANY"

Episode No. 8: "Sally Suffers a Setback"

Sally sat staring at her desktop, drumming her fingers in irritation.

"You look discouraged about something."

Sally looked up to see Elaine standing in her office doorway. "Oh, it's just that I'm getting spoiled around here."

Elaine came in and seated herself across from Sally. "What happened?"

"I went to a Civic Theater board meeting last night. It was a zoo. No agenda. No organization. Everybody going off in all directions. I wanted to knock their heads together."

"I know the feeling," said Elaine. "Ever since Frank got us to see how effective committees *can* be, it's very frustrating to see how badly run they so often are."

"It's a bloody shame," said Sally. "It was supposed to be just a short meeting to approve a raise in the amount we pay directors—at least that's what the president said when she called me on the phone. When I got there, we had to wait around for 45 minutes before everyone showed up. Then we spent an hour deciding whether or not to fire the business manager—with half the people not wanting to hurt the guy's feelings. We spent more time talking about next year's productions—*next* year's, mind you, and we haven't started this year's yet. I walked out after three hours, and we still hadn't got to the director's pay issue.''

"Nobody there gets a conspirator's pin, I take it."

Sally looked across at her friend, a fiendish glimmer in her eye. "Not yet, but *I* volunteered to set up a special meeting to talk about the business manager, to analyze what he's done for the past year and set strategy for this coming season. *I'm* going to be setting up the agenda, and they're about to learn all there is to know about Decision Audits. Before this year is out, there are going to be coffeepots on every board member. I guarantee it."

Elaine stood and shied away from Sally in mock terror. "You're scary, you know that? Today Omnibus. Tomorrow the world. Are you sure that the human race is ready for all this organization?"

PART III. ROLES TO MAKE THINGS GO RIGHT

Effective decision making cannot be accomplished solely by application of rules. Neither rules nor facts "speak for themselves." Rules need to be applied within a context, and they need to be applied by individuals in that context. Hence, the next two parts of the book deal with roles and contexts.

In Part III we will focus upon roles and, in particular, the role of the Chair, the role of the Member, and the role of the Staffer or person who is paid to assist a committee in carrying out its decision-making functions. The final chapter will look at the role repertoire or role ensemble that individuals in the committee and meetings business must carry around. We will also consider some ways in which flexibility and interchange ability can be facilitated.

Most of us have only conventional understanding about group decision-making roles. As we indicated earlier in this book, people generally have little training for some of the major roles they will need to undertake. The role of Chair is certainly one of those. It is not at all unusual when one of us becomes the Chair of a committee or board to ask a colleague, "What should I do? How shall I act? What are my responsibilities?" The best that our friends have to offer is a copy of Robert's *Rules of Order*.

Most of us feel intuitively and by observation that there's more to being a Chair than generalship over a set of marching motions. Yet precious little information is likely to be forthcoming. We've all sat in meetings that seem to have run with uncommon smoothness, where the Chair was knowledgeable and seemed to make all the right moves. We may very well have marveled at the skill we observed and attributed that skill to luck, chance, or the moon's being in the right phase. We are equally certain that there is no way we could acquire such skill through education and training. The truth is that anyone can be a good Chair, and everyone should be.

Similarly, we have had very little training in the simplified role of being a committee Member. Doesn't everybody know how to be a Member? Isn't it "doin' what comes naturally"? It most certainly is not. And those who have observed group interaction can attest to the fact that people are singularly unaware of important themes and streams running through decision-making groups to which they contribute. Nevertheless, as a general principle, people are simply unaware of their own impact. Members make suggestions, the nature of which, if implemented, could radically alter the purpose, the function, even the nature of the group. Yet, they seem blithely unconcerned about the havoc they wreak. Members chime in with "By the way, it just occurred to me," and "Somebody mentioned that," with relatively little thought about the impact of their queries and suggestions on the group itself, and on the decision-making process. Hence, a greater degree of sensitivity is required for both group Members and Chairs.

It is also the case that many of us at various times are assigned the job of "staffing" committees. When that happens, we become a committee Staffer. What is a Staffer? It is a person who is assigned to assist the committee in carrying out its role. Often, that person is also paid, but in some instances the Staffer is a volunteer, a student, a loaned executive, or someone along those lines (although, as a loaned executive, the Staffer continues to receive pay from the company of origin). Staffers typically are not *Members* of groups; thus a role alteration must occur when one plays this role, especially if one plays it in the presence of friends and acquaintances.

Perhaps the best way to think about committee roles is to use Erving Goffman's notion of "dramaturgy." In his book *The Presentation of Self in Everyday Life,* Goffman asked us to consider seriously Shakespeare's dictum that all the world's a stage and all the men and women on it merely players. If we were actually putting on a play or a skit before colleagues and friends, we would do our best to play the roles assigned us seriously and well. Group activities can be regarded as playlike in nature. Thus, we become actorlike in nature. Yet we're continually slipping out of our role, changing the script, modifying the script to suit ourselves. While scripts can certainly be developed in process, as the "living theater" movement demonstrates, there needs to be an overall framework within which that development occurs. It is for this reason that we need to pay special attention to committee and decision-making roles.

9
The Role of the Chair

"And now, if you please, I'm ready to try"
—W. S. Gilbert, *Trial by Jury*

The role of the Chair is one of the most difficult in the committee process. In part this is so because of the complexities inherent in the role itself. In part, too, people attribute to the role of Chair the good things or bad things that happen in the committee process. This unilateral description is part of our individualistic mentality. If something goes right, somebody must be responsible for it. If something goes wrong, it has to be somebody's fault. It often takes the form: "Any credit goes to me; any blame goes to you."

Time and again, as we have worked with decision-making groups in improving their process, the Members have indicated that they feel lack of adequate Chairship is a central, if not *the* central problem. Almost no one ascribes any blame or fault (or any expectations at all for that matter) to the committee Members. It's the Chair who is supposed to motivate, crystallize, develop, encourage, nudge, punish, and so on, a group of essentially neutral human beings to achievement and accomplishment.

This perspective, however faulty, is wonderfully reassuring. It avoids the need to recognize that for every problematic Chair, there's an equally problematic committee.

Contrary to popular belief, Members are not supposed to be neutral. They are supposed to participate actively with the Chair in the accomplishment of the organizational goals, as we'll see in Chapter 10. Here, our concern is with the role, or rather the constellation of important roles that define the Chair.

KEY SUBROLES OF THE CHAIR

While there is a sharing of many responsibilities by the Chair and the Members, there are a number specifically designated to the Chair. Some of these are unique, with the most significant overlying four essential, interconnected roles:

1. The Role of Leader
2. The Role of Administrator
3. The Role of Spokesperson
4. The Role of Meeting Head

Let's consider each of these in turn.

The Role of Leader

The role of the Leader is a complicated one. The Chair has to be far enough ahead of the group to point the direction in which the group might go and offer models of alternative missions for group consideration. At the same time, the Chair cannot be too far ahead because at too great a distance leadership gets lost over the horizon. Like all other tasks that relate to group roles, it is continually a matter of balance and posture.

The Leader role has several specific subroles that we'll mention shortly. Two themes, however, are constant throughout. One is intellectual leadership. The other is interpersonal leadership.

Intellectual leadership involves being an "idea champion" (Daft and Bradshaw, 1980), taking the kernel of one suggestion and the kernel of another and providing support and enthusiasm for them. People who work to increase the supply of ideas within the decision-making group structure know that for every good idea there are many not so good ones that the good idea depends on. The Chair must seek, therefore, to provide a center for new and fresh ideas and approaches. This intellectual aspect, incidentally, does not mean that the Chair must forever be spouting original suggestions. Indeed, it's the support for and, perhaps, the blending of new approaches that winds up being the most useful example of the Leader. Consider the orchestra metaphor we've used before. The orchestra conductor does not need to supply innovative new techniques for every instrument. He or she *does* need to be receptive to experimenting with those techniques in rehearsal and performance. It is that supportive posture, through which a suggestion or two can be made, that is crucial.

While intellectual leadership involves the blending of ideas, interpersonal leadership involves the blending of people. This practice is what is normally thought of as the "process" aspect of group leadership. It's a crucial part of that leadership (though without intellectual support, the fact that people feel valued and cohesive does not really lead to any productive result).

As an interpersonal leader, the Chair becomes the supporter of the *person* rather than of the *idea*. Put another way, the idea recedes, and the person becomes foremost. With the Chair as intellectual leader, the person recedes, and the idea becomes foremost. There will be an ebb and flow of each during the course of a meeting, but an overall balance between the two is essential.

The tasks associated with these two subroles require somewhat different skills for each. The individual who is adept at conceptual leadership may not be the person who is most skilled at interpersonal integration. The reverse is also true. It is important, therefore, for committee Members to assist the Chair by playing some of the Chair roles that an individual Chair may not be able to play. This is one important reason why committee passivity is so problematic.

But there is a task that only the Chair can perform: the *blending* of ideas and people. As ideas are suggested, the Chair's knowledge of individual committee members helps the chair to assign further exploration to those most interested and competent, and to make links with those who have additional and needed knowledge but are quiet. In essence, the blending of people and ideas is the ultimate expression of effective Chairship, just as the blending of effective musicians and music is the hallmark of a good conductor.

This blending of ideas and people characterizes the overall job of the Chair as Leader. Let's now look at some of the more specific activities.

Being a Model of Committee Behavior.   The Chair serves as a model of behavior for the committee Members. Consider the rules we talked about before. If the Chair doesn't pay attention to them, certainly the Members won't. The Chair's actions are taken, like it or not, as a signal of what is appropriate and permissible within the particular committee. If the Chair feels that it is all right to attack and criticize Members, so will other Members. If the Chair feels that it is permissible to ignore time deadlines and other committee conventions, so will the Members. This signal or model role that the Chair plays is an important hidden influence on what kinds of activities the committee Members take to be acceptable and which ones they consider unacceptable.

Synthesizing Contributions.   The Chair is a *statesman* not a *partisan*. Accepting the Chair role means that an individual sets aside particular pet issues, gives up the virtuoso performer role, and seeks to be one who pulls together the contributions of others. This may be one of the hardest tasks for the Chair to accomplish. Many of us don't succeed at it. Instead, we use the Chair as a platform from which to advance our own ideas, often to the detriment of those advanced by others.

The Chair role demands the blending of contributions so that a range of different aspects of involvement is facilitated, so that a range of different issues contained within a different, larger issue is brought to the fore. If the Chair does not act in this manner, acting instead in a peremptory and unsympathetic way, one that does not reveal an understanding of people and issues, then the Chair is not effectively taking the important leadership role.

Exercising Responsibility.   Few issues cause the Chair more perplexity and difficulty than that of responsibility. On the one hand, Chairs tell us, they want other people to do things; they want involvement. On the other, they claim that people never do come forward, that there is a real hesitancy on the part of Members to contribute. Chairs often take the view that accepting the Chair simply means that they are asked to do all the work. When we talk with Members, a similar but reverse story emerges: Members want to do more, they claim, yet the Chair does it all. Often, heated confrontation occurs with sharp differences of viewpoint concerning who *is* taking the initiative and who *should* be taking it. There is merit to the arguments of both sides, but often it is a case of "failed role transition" on the part of the Chair that leads the Chair into problems.

If, like a cellist named Toscanini, you move from the role of player to conductor of a symphony orchestra, then your job with respect to the orchestra changes. In the same way, it's not appropriate for the Chair now to seek to play all the instruments, to become a one-man band, collapsing after each performance in sweaty exhaustion. Rather, the work of the Chair is to facilitate the doing of the task, *not to do the task itself*.

This distinction may seem fuzzy, but it's a fundamental part of the essence of leadership. The Chair in a Leader role must be supportive of, must persuade, must encourage Members to do the jobs they've agreed to do. A famous administrator, when asked what he did with his time, replied: "I spend 90% of my time getting people to do what they should be doing in the first place." Most experienced managers at any level would echo that statement.

The question really isn't whether people *should* do what they are supposed to do—of course they should, and in due course most of them will. The committee world, however, like the rest of our world is one of competing pressures and claims; and it is important for the Chair to be a representative pressure on the individual but not to do so in a way that becomes a negative incentive. For the individual who feels that the Chair will trap him, lord it over him in cases of committee failure, there is no incentive to comply, only to escape. Yet it is difficult for the Chair not to feel irritation, annoyance, or anger at having to be involved continually in an encouraging and supportive posture. We can recognize the legitimacy of that feeling without endorsing its expression; and the reason that a tempered expression is crucial is that the venting of anger under these kinds of situations tends to produce negative reinforcement of individuals in the accomplishment of their tasks. In a very real sense that's why we have Chairs, to provide the kind of encouragement and support to people that they need to get a job done that they've agreed to do. We don't appoint a Chair to do the job, anymore than we appoint an orchestra conductor to play all the instruments. Chairs must recognize that this kind of frustration is inherent in the job. It's not a matter of bad will or hostile individuals (though sometimes this is surely the case). Rather, it's a question of individual Members seeking to meet the demands of this and other groups, of home and family, and so on, and being not quite able—as many of us aren't—to get them all to come together in exactly the way they would hope.

There is another, but closely related, potential trouble spot for the Chair, centering on the way in which delegated tasks are performed. Most of us at any given level of our organization or our work life have a certain style that we like to use to accomplish tasks: reports should be written thus and so, procedures for accounting should be handled in specific ways, even our driving should be handled in carefully defined ways. We have a tendency to feel that these ways represent, if not the only ways (though we secretly often believe that), certainly the very best ones. As we delegate, then, a tendency develops to insist that subordinates, committee Members, others, do the job exactly as we would do it. All too often we define that way as the "right" way, and such a definition begs for trouble. There are, in fact, many ways to skin a cat just as there are many ways to do almost anything.

Some of those ways are doubtless better than others. But there is almost always a group of ways at the top that are, relatively speaking, equal. And even if one appears to be better, the distance between that better one and an alternate that will get the job done adequately may very well be insignificant. Chairs waste altogether too much time trying to get those who have been delegated tasks to do them in exactly the way that the Chair would have done were he or she in that spot. Often, as a result, Chairs collapse in a fit of exasperation and say, "I'll have to do it myself," demeaning the integrity and motivation of the person who did it, and humiliating him or her in task performance.

There are situations that occur in which the task is not performed well. It's been our observation, however, that those are substantially fewer than situations in which the style of task performance differs from that of the Chair and *ipso facto* is called "not performing the task well." To an outside observer, the difference seems slight. It's important, therefore, for you, as the Chair, to remember: in the delegating process, delegate decisions about the way in which the task is performed within a fairly broad range of competence and look very closely and doubtfully at your own definition of competence when it becomes an issue.

The Role of Administrator

A second major subrole that the Chair has is that of Administrator. This role is often performed by or heavily shared with the Staff person, or individual assigned to handle the committee responsibilities on a paid basis, if such a person exists. Often, though, there is no person assigned to handle the job. In that case, responsibility for seeing to it that the job is accomplished falls on the Chair.

Being the committee Administrator means seeing to it that all the range of preparatory and planning tasks requisite to successful meeting activity are performed. In its meeting-related activity, administration means seeing to it that the meeting room is available, that the arrangement of the room is satisfactory for the upcoming meeting, and that all the equipment—overhead projectors, tape players, movie projectors, video tape players, and so on—that is needed for the session at hand has been reserved or made available. Countless hours are wasted by Chairs or Members in a last-minute scurrying to get the room, to double back and get equipment needed, and to set up the room, taking care of all trivia that should have been seen to earlier. It would be considered an act of rudeness to ask a guest we've invited to a formal dinner party to set the table. We would also be a bit shocked if the orchestra conductor at a major concert turned to us and said, "The orchestra hasn't had a lot of chance to play this particular piece, so we're going to rehearse it a bit, and then we'll play it for you." We feel that such activities should be handled before the people arrive. The Chair needs to see to the accomplishment of these tasks. If the meeting is going to have coffee, then the Chair needs to take responsibility for having the coffee available or doing what needs to be done to get it there.

Of course, these tasks are not always directly completed by the Chair, nor should they be. Often, at the direction of the Chair, the Staff person sees to it that these kinds of things are taken care of. They remain, nevertheless, the responsibility of the Chair. We've all sat through too many meetings in which the Chair has blamed everyone but him- or herself—the secretary didn't do this, the staff didn't do that—until the litanies of blame have become tiresome and irritating.

The Chair must become involved in administrative activities well before the meeting. As the meeting ends, the Chair makes a note about the items that require follow-up. Some of these might be issues that arose during the discussion period or in relationship to one of the items. They might relate to an announcement someone made. A particular action taken may require implemental next steps. These become grist for the mill under the Rule of Halves; these items, plus others, are pulled together around the midpoint of the intervening period, as suggested by the Rule of Halves. The Chair will work with the Staff person or the Executive Director to get the kinds of information and people needed in order to pursue or answer the issues and questions that are on the upcoming agenda. Sometimes this means making several calls, asking people if they intend to be present, if they have their report, what their thinking is on this or that. The Chair must reach out proactively, seeking to find out what people's problems and concerns are and what they think about specific issues. Then the process begins of blending that and other information into the agenda for the next meeting.

What's involved here is combining the proposed items with the proposed or needed information and then making a final decision on the items, based on the availability of people, documents, and other kinds of information, Suppose, for example, that the ABC report is going to be discussed, but for this upcoming meeting, Sam, who has been deeply involved with that particular report, cannot be present. It's probably unwise to put it on the agenda with the notion that Sam *might* show up at the last minute. As we've tried to stress throughout, things that pop up at the last minute—whether people or ideas—are not in a format amenable to serious consideration. But, it requires proactive work to find out whether or not Sam will be present.

In other cases, more than information is needed. Arm twisting and extraction may be called for. Consider Fred, who has had the responsibility for reporting on his analysis of the transportation costs and can't, for some reason, seem to let it go. Here, the Chair or others need to set some limits and enforce them.

There may be a range of special details, as well, things like double-checking the room for smoke-eating equipment so that nonsmokers can be protected. Special attention may need to be given to any handicapped Members, to special scheduling needs of individuals, and so on. These are the kinds of things that, if completed, will make the meeting go much better.

In the course of carrying out these administrative duties, the Chair or Executive learns a lot about what issues might arise, how people are feeling, what their orientations and perspectives are. There is, thus, in some sense a double benefit to this kind of activity. The first benefit is the accomplishment of the job itself. The second is a kind of intelligence function that begins to funnel information into the eyes and ears of the committee leadership. This information becomes indispensable in their thinking about what issues may be coming up and preparing the organization to anticipate demands, requests, and areas of interest, rather than simply waiting for something to happen.

The Role of the Spokesperson

The Chair is the Spokesperson of the committee. In this respect the Chair performs a function not appropriately undertaken by the staff. As a Spokesperson, the Chair represents the committee at official functions and seeks to reflect the committee's views in a balanced fashion. Of course, individuals who are outside the committee expect the Chair as Leader to perform these functions. It is to the Chair that questions from external sources are addressed, and it is from the Chair that these external individuals want to learn about committee activity.

The Chair should be careful to present a balanced view—this is another aspect of the Statesman role. It would certainly be easy to vent one's spleen, particularly given the temporary satisfaction of an understanding reporter or information service/PR person. We tend not to have enough opportunity to talk out our committee frustrations and to get other views about them when we're in the Chair role. Intemperate or particularistic statements, however, are likely to haunt us later. On especially difficult items, then, or those of high public importance or interest, the Chair should initiate discussion with the committee about the nature of the public release desired for particular pieces of business.

As a practical matter, this does not happen very often. Most of us do not have the occasion to deal with the press, radio, or television on a regular basis. But we've all had it sometimes; and when it happens, if it happens without any preparation, the effects can be startling and embarrassing. Nothing quite matches the sense of total misery that goes with watching yourself spout garbled idiocy on the six o'clock news—unless it's the voices of your smirking and giggling friends on the phone immediately afterward, calling to tell you that they have just seen you on television.

The Spokesperson role, particularly as it relates to dealing with the media, should recognize that the media have no inherent responsibility to be fair. We would like them to be fair. We hope they'll be fair. But charges of "unfair press" have littered the halls of public figures as long as the Republic has stood. Therefore, one must take care to craft statements that are only minimally liable to misinterpretation and cutting.

Dealing with the media, however, is not the only aspect of the Spokesperson's role. Simply representing the group before public bodies (e.g., city councils), boards of directors, executive committees, and so on, becomes a part of that role, too. These duties are seldom as dramatic as the media encounters, but they are often as fateful. It's part of the way that the committee implements some of its decisions; that is, by communicating them to outside groups who must then, themselves, take action. It's also part of the way that the committee gets information—in such discussions intelligence about the way the community is leaning, what its attitudes are, and so on, can also be communicated.

Finally, the Chair can serve as the Spokesperson for absent Members. The whole process of securing information and making assessments of its adequacy with respect to agenda development permits the Chair to find out if, for example, some individuals cannot be present, and if they have a point of view they would like conveyed. This can frequently be done quite successfully. In fact, some people find they are more effective and more influential when they are not present.

The Role of Meeting Head

Finally, the Chair takes responsibility for being the head of the meeting. This has been put last because it has so often been put first. Indeed, it is frequently and erroneously seen as the only essential responsibility of the Chair.

Just as the meeting is the product of a series of preparations, being the Meeting Head emerges as a role based upon, and drawing from other roles. One simply does not stroll in and chair a meeting, any more than one strolls in and conducts an orchestra, or strolls in and gives a dinner party. Rather, whatever the appearance, there has been preparation and development. Nonetheless, while it is an essential prologue to Meeting Headship, don't assume that preparation ensures the success of any meeting without additional work. It most certainly does not. There are a number of things that the Chair needs to attend to within the meeting itself.

Provide Orderly Procedure: Equality for Persons, Equity for Issues. First among these matters is some insistence upon orderly procedure. We have suggested a set of rules that are as useful as any. Other rules may be preferred. That's fine. It's not particular rules but the absence of the enforcement of any rules that so often leads to chaos that masquerades for meetings. The key point in running a meeting is that there must be uniformity and equality with respect to the membership and equity with respect to the issues.

Equality of membership means that all Members are viewed as being equal. All Members have an equal right to be heard on any issue. Sometimes their contribution is not as salient as one might wish, but such an assessment provides no justification for ignoring individuals.

Equity with respect to issues means that issues are differentially treated as a function of their importance. Larger issues are given more time. Smaller, less important ones are given less time.

Unfortunately, and all too often, the actual practices of equity and equality get reversed. We have issue equality and Member inequity. All issues are given the same time while more and less important individuals are treated differentially within the meeting.

In the matter of Member equality, the need to temper overparticipation and enhance underparticipation is especially important. Some individuals are big talkers. We know that, and, probably, they know that. It's important for the Chair to temper overparticipation, usually doing so via the announced need to permit time for others to speak who have not yet had a chance to express themselves. Thus, the enhancing of underparticipation can be used as the precipitating reason at least for tempering overparticipation.

Just as some individuals are quite unrestrained, others are quite inhibited and need more than the usual amount of encouragement to contribute to the group. The fact that individuals don't volunteer information on a particular point should not be taken as evidence that they have nothing to say. Often, they have a lot to say. Very frequently, it's of high quality. But it's important for the Chair to give people the kinds of permission they need to participate. A skilled Chair may say, "Well, Thelma, I know you have a particular interest in this issue. What do you think?" or, "Sam, you and I were talking the other day about this point, and you made some interesting suggestions. Maybe you'd be willing to share them with us." These kinds of interactions are not the sole responsibility of the Chair. All Members should share with the Chair the burden of shaping the discussion. Members are more likely to do that, however, if the Chair takes the lead by example, and models some occasions of tempering overparticipation and enhacing underparticipation.

Crystallize Discussion at Crucial Points.   Timing in meetings is crucial, as it is in all important matters. Chairs need to time the point at which they crystallize discussions or suggest crystallization so that they convey just the right tone to the group. That's likely to be a matter of judgment, but here's a good rule of thumb: *When everyone has had a chance to speak at least once on the issue, the Chair should take that point as one of the trial crystallization junctures.* Crystallization may not be possible then, and another round of discussion and consideration may be required. However, the point of crystallization is not always to conclude issues (that is, "crystallization and conclusion"); sometimes it is to bring into focus a particular group position and to prepare the way for another round of discussions that will, it is hoped, continue productive deliberation on the issue.

If that point at which everyone has contributed at least once is missed, and some others begin to talk, then experience suggests that many more will want to get their "turn" in before crystallization occurs. Hence, one must seize the moment. If that opportunity is missed, one must wait until the next appropriate chance.

Crystallization, then, is the effort to bring together the ideas expressed by the Members in the most useful possible form. The integrity of that effort is sustained by the Statesman role, since Members must not think that the Chair is somehow secretly using the process of crystallization as a way of exclusively advancing his or her own personal goals. Obviously, personal goals of various individuals will be advanced; but there has to be a prima facie public validity to the crystallization, or it will be attacked as a false one.

In a decision-making group, where the responsibility for decision-making rests with the group, the Chair should seek to offer a sample or candidate conclusion. More process-oriented individuals hate to do this. They will say, "Are we ready to conclude?" or, "Can we conclude?," but they will never offer a hypothetical conclusion in the form, "I think we're at this point and let's go ahead unless I hear differently from you." Offering such a conclusion is risky, but it's well worth doing because many individuals have an aversion to taking on that kind of responsibility.

Use Authority to Promote Progress.   Within the role of Meeting Head, the Chair seeks to use his or her authority to move things along. That's part of the reason for having times on the Agenda. The Chair can refer to those times as a way of facilitating the interaction process around particular issues. The Chair tries to keep the process moving at an appropriate speed.

The Chair seeks to protect the weaker from attack by the stronger Members. Often, this occurs within the meeting context; and even though the Chair may agree with the attack, joining in it is bad modeling. It must, therefore, be avoided.

The Chair, for a variety of reasons, has extra authority beyond that of others in the group. Sometimes this authority comes, as it does in the case of the host of a dinner party, from having extended an invitation. Sometimes, as in the case of the symphony orchestra conductor, it comes through a combination of selection and competence. In still other cases, it is given by the group alone. The source of authority is important in thinking about how you should carry out your role as Chair.

It is essentially true that the greater the amount of organizational authority invested in the Chair, the more difficult Chairship may become. It is, after all, quite natural to fall back on authority rather than to engage in leadership for the accomplishment of social purpose. Leadership can be facilitated by authority—and, certainly, the authority's views are given special consideration. Generally speaking, and especially in complex organizations, use of authority is rarely the preferred or the successful way to solve problems. While decisions can be achieved by fiat, carrying them out cannot. As authority becomes authoritarian, resistance and eventually sabotage can arise. Paradoxically, the more the Chair insists on authority in the group—and the more authoritarian she or he becomes—the more resistance there is likely to develop within the group, and the more authority the Chair will find it necessary to use. This upward escalation can often lead to open warfare between the Chair and the group and among Members of the group.

The central principle to remember is that you must depend upon others for the accomplishment of goals, if not their selection. Some degree of commitment to those goals, therefore, is absolutely essential if they are to be carried out efficiently and effectively, if the spirit of the decision to be implemented rather than just its letter.

PRELIMINARY CONSIDERATIONS

The Chair role is an important one. This is obvious both from our discussion here and from our conventional understanding. Thus it's important to give some thought to what kinds of things might be needed for successful performance *before* you accept a Chairship role.

Deciding to become a Chair is equivalent in many respects to the process of evaluating a new job possibility. There's a period of mutual appraisal. The candidate Chair may find things that he or she thinks necessary for successful accomplishment. Those must be stated as part of the original negotiations. Otherwise, promises may not be fulfilled, answers to concerns may not be forthcoming, resources may not be supplied, and so on.

Staff/Resources

The candidate Chair needs to consider what kinds of staff assistance and resources (including financial and material) are needed for the accomplishment of the task at hand. Those need to be made a condition of acceptance.

Sometimes very little is needed. Other times a very substantial allocation of resources is required. If those kinds of assessments are not made early and stated firmly, one is likely to be given a job with less than the necessary equipment. Failure under those conditions is not mitigated by one's saying, "Well, I tried to get the kinds of things we needed. . . ."

Time

A time analysis should be made, both of the candidate Chair's time and of the time the job will take. The two should be compared.

In doing this analysis you should keep in mind that those who are trying to entice you into the Chair role have every motivation to minimize or to lie about the time required. We have all discovered at one time or another the extent of the "fraud in the inducement," learning this to our infinite regret after we have taken a job. Remember, here as in other places it's always much easier to decline intially than to resign later.

Political Assessment

You will need to review the nature of the group, itself: Who is there and why? What kind of group is it? What is it, as well as can be ascertained, that the Members want? What is their individual and collective stance? What does a reading of the group suggest?

Here, again, potential Chairs may feel that they have this aspect well in hand, especially if they have been a Member of the group. We are talking about a different kind of position, however, with a different kind of perspective. It is useful to take a new look at the group. Review the individual Members. See what kinds of strengths and weaknesses are present. If special or unique individual (Member) competencies need to be present for the accomplishment of the task, their absence may well doom the effort to failure from the outset. Additions or replacements may be needed for any prospect of success.

Self Assessment

Like it or not, the appointment of anyone to a Chair role is a signal to the committee itself, to a meeting group, and to a larger environment. It is imperative for the Chair nominee or designate to understand what is being signalled by the offer of Chairship. Self knowledge may be the most difficult kind of knowledge to acquire. Outside sources of such knowledge are not entirely reliable because here, too, people may be less than candid. Consider, for example, designation of a female Chair where there has never before been a woman in the position. Should she ask if her gender figured in the nomination, she is very likely to receive the answer "Certainly not!"—an answer that will almost surely be somewhat, if not totally, false.

The reason that such knowledge is important is that the signal is certainly understood by others if not by oneself. It governs at least in part the way that others react to the Chair. Thus, if you do not understand the symbolic meaning of the appointment, then you do not have the knowledge and flexibility to carry out the role. We are in no way suggesting that you have to agree with the symbolism; you simply have to be aware of it.

Such self knowledge may come from introspection. It is also useful to have someone else's view. Here a system of organizational mentorship is very useful and important. Whereas such an arrangement is not characteristic of American business, Pascale and Athos mention that it is an important element in Japanese companies. We do have an example like it, however, in the clinical relationship existing among therapists as they assist each other in carrying out their therapeutic work. Psychiatrists, psychologists, and other health professionals will always have another mental health professional with whom they review cases, who can alert them to some of the perils of things they might be doing, and who can provide some suggestions about alternative techniques. Whatever else it does, that relationship provides a way for the therapist to sit down and talk with a knowledgeable professional about case progress.

Executives and Chairs have no such person available. It might be wise to seek one out. The mentor should be older and from a different part of the company or organization. This assures knowledgeable yet removed observation. Then, as issues of potential Chairship (or any other issues, for that matter) arise, the mentor can provide a discussion and a perspective that the individual, him- or herself, may lack. This is so simply because it is very hard to see ourselves as others see us.

Mandate in Writing

The last thing that you, the candidate Chair, should check out before finally agreeing to serve is the mandate. Often mandates of particular committees or purposes of particular meetings are vague and mysterious. For committees, at least, the mandate should be produced in writing. There are several reasons why this is a good idea.

First, the ambiguity of mission expectations can be reduced when put on paper. Hidden expectations and important nuances often become more distinct.

Second, once that clarity is achieved, the Chair designate may wish to negotiate to some degree about the mandate. Mandates are political documents. It may be politically useful to the potential Chair to have something included or omitted. That negotiation is very difficult if one has already accepted the position.

Third, it's imperative that you provide a copy of this document to the Members of the committee. Committee Members after all, deserve to know what it is that they are being asked to do.

CONCLUSION

The role of the Chair is complex and multifaceted. The suggestions made here represent a beginning, but only that, of serious thinking about role performance. It's useful to keep in mind that none of us is taught how to be a Chair. When that topic comes up, if ever, it is too often approached in a minimalistic way. From the point of view of mastery of Robert's *Rules of Order,* for example, and as we try to carry out a meeting according to Robert's *Rules,* we find these rules don't really help us much.[1] This doesn't mean that such rules aren't useful. They certainly are, in their proper place. But they should not be a substitute for a more detailed, broader-gauge discussion of the role of the Chair. This chapter provides a start in that direction.

"GENERAL COMPANY"

Episode #9: "M.E.E.T. Roles On"

It was progress review time as the principal M.E.E.T. conspirators gathered around Frank's coffeepot.

"I don't know how much longer I'm going to be able to hold off on a report to Bill," Elaine said. "He's pleased with what's been going on, I'm sure; but he's also getting a little suspicious. He keeps telling me that things are just going too well, which means something has to be wrong."

Frank and Sally both laughed. "We're doing well,

---

[1] There are times when you need Robert's *Rules,* though, and the League of Women Voters has an excellent, small, pamphlet-style version that can be purchased in multiple copies quite inexpensively. Not only can everyone follow the rules in this form, but everyone can (and should) have a copy. Providing everyone with a copy means that all have access to rules, not just a few. You can contact the League office near you or in New York, or see the reprinted version in F. M. Cox, et al., *Tactics and Techniques of Community Practice.*

I've got to admit," Frank said, "but we're still only about halfway through."

"Oh?" said Sally. "You mean there's more?"

"There sure is," said Frank. "Good meetings require a focus on some rules and a focus on some roles. We've accomplished the first part by getting our recruited co-conspirators to begin implementing some of the rules we've been spouting. Now we've got to finish the job."

"Whatever you say, coach," Elaine said.

"Right," said Sally. "I've still got a whole pocketful of pins."

"O.K.," said Frank. "Our next step is to get people to perform differently in meetings. That, by the way, is why everything connected with chairing a meeting is so important."

"Well," said Sally, "I can tell you that since I've stopped sticking my two cents' worth in from the Chair's spot, things in my meetings have sure have been going a lot more smoothly."

"It's tough being a Chair," said Frank, "but there's something that just might be harder."

"What's that?" Elaine asked.

Frank looked at the two of them enigmatically. "Being a Member."

10
The Role of the Member

"Strephon's a Member of Parliament, running amuck at all abuses."
—W. S. Gilbert, *Iolanthe*

Who, you might very well ask, needs any kind of direction to be a *Member* of any kind of group? Surely, that's the kind of thing that comes naturally. Although large numbers of people believe that it does, a great deal of observation suggests that it does not. The rudiments of Membership do not simply spring to us. They need to be thought about, absorbed, practiced. The purpose of this chapter is to provide some initial considerations.

To begin with, Membership involves a mutuality of goals: one's own Member goals on the one hand as personal statements, and group goals on the other. This has been a historical dilemma for Members to resolve. A proper balance has often been illusive. Consider, for example, the role of "representative." Suppose that you are a representative from a department or a division of a company to a larger corporate-wide group. Is it your obligation to carry out the "instructions" of those who selected you, or should your orders now be set by the board and your own judgment be the sole, guiding principle? Obviously this question cannot be answered in its entirety one way or the other, but it represents the kind of dilemma that Members must think about.

Members also need to be aware of group process. For example, many people are unaware that the silent Member of the group is considered by other Members to be negative and hostile.

The silent one is often surprised and angry or hurt when others make the judgment about him or her. Yet, the techniques for neutralizing that feeling are simple. Just an indication that one is not quite up to snuff at a particular time is often enough to diffuse hostile reactions. Simple as such neutralization is, though, it is often not used; and that failure to communicate is due in almost every case to a lack of knowledge.

Members often sit back and let the Chair do all the work. As important as the Chair is, that strategy is certain to assure a lackluster decision-making group, and probably poor-quality decisions as well.

There are many kinds of role considerations that the Member must take into account. Some of the most important of these are touched on in this chapter.

ASSESSMENT PROCESS

The same assessment that we discussed at the end of the preceding chapter with respect to Chairs may be applied to Members as well. Questions of time, political assessment, the nature of the other Members, and so on, become a useful checklist that the Member can keep as a set of bases to touch. The implication is that if an appropriate type of arrangement cannot be made, one does not join the group. There are, of course, situations in which not joining is not an available option. For example, the Member may be simply a Member of a staff group and therefore obligated to attend certain types of meeting sessions. In that situation, the suggested checklist may become a set of considerations that will help him or her have an additional perspective on the committee or group, its needs, and its problems.

ENFORCEMENT OF COMMITTEE RULES

The rules developed in the last section do not enforce themselves, nor can they be enforced completely by the Chair. Rather, there must be joint participation of Chair and Membership in their enforcement. Committee Members can seek to follow the Rule of Halves, can press for an agenda that is written and comprehensive, can press for content minutes, and in general use those rules as goals if they are not currently in operation.

PREPARATION FOR CONTENT DISCUSSION

It is of crucial importance that the Member prepare well for upcoming meetings; and, yet—and this point is related to the one just made—if there is not a sense of integrity, if that preparation is not made worthwhile through discussion, then there are systematic disincentives for doing one's "homework." For this reason, the Member not only needs to do homework but to act in a supportive way to a set of rules that make doing the homework worthwhile.

Appropriate Participation

Within the meeting structure, itself, the Member is responsible for appropriate participation. Generally, the rule of thumb that is useful here is to participate at the rate at which others in the group are also participating. This means that in some high-participation groups, a particular individual has to contribute a bit more. For low-participation groups, it means that individuals may need to temper their participation a bit. Certainly, though, failure to participate is unlikely to be acceptable and may have negative fallout. The overparticipator should also observe his or her own behavior and temper it.

As issues come up, the Member needs to select those about which he feels most strongly, allocating his participation differentially within the meeting structure. Although we have talked about equality of treatment, equality does not extend to overparticipation on each issue. If there is one issue about which a Member has a bit more to say, he may temper his participation on other issues and, in effect, engage in inter-issue borrowing. Committees and meetings will usually tolerate some of this. So if you have not participated a great deal on two issues, you may usually take extra time on another issue that you feel more strongly about.

Alternatively, Members are sometimes surprised to realize that they have wasted their committee influence by overparticipating earlier in the meeting, then finding group tolerance for them very low on something quite important to them.

Overall, then, participation needs thought. It needs to be approached in a considered fashion.

There is one final aspect of appropriate participation that deserves attention. Often, Members will create problems for the group without providing any way for the group to help them out. For example, the Member who says, "I am worried about this idea (or proposal or plan) . . . " and stops there, invites the other Members to play Find-the-Problem. Not only can this be time-consuming, it is time not usefully spent. Generally, the Member who raises an issue has a responsibility to offer at least a range of suggestions or directions that would resolve his concerns.

SERVICE TO THE COMMITTEE
OUTSIDE THE MEETINGS

The committee Member does a good deal of work outside the meetings. Obviously, preparing is part of it, but that's not the focus here. Rather, the Member is on the alert for information and perspectives that can help the committee achieve its goals. Many of us simply tune out once the meeting ends, and never turn on again until we sit down to the next meeting. Unfortunately, the kind of perspective leaves a lot to be desired because the kinds of information the committee needs often come to the fore when the committee is not in session. The Member needs to be alert to, to be sensitive to, and sometimes pursue, then, the kinds of things that the committee might want to know.

Sometimes, the pursuit of this knowledge requires some activism and follow-up. Other times the Member needs to pick up the phone and alert the Chair or Staffer. It becomes imperative that you, as a committee Member, follow through.

RESPECT FOR THE COMMITTEE'S PURPOSE

Once you have accepted a position on a committee, then a degree of policy loyalty is important. You should not run down or criticize the committee outside the committee itself. This is often a difficult task. You may very well disagree emphatically with the decisions made by the committee. The desire to portray oneself as a person who has the right answers and others as "dopes," however, should be strongly resisted. Like it or not, we are all known by the company we keep. If we manage to persuade the world that we are keeping the company of fools, it should come as no surprise to us when the world, for its part, regards us as foolish.

As a committee Member, you should always seek to maintain a posture of integrity. Of course you can indicate that there are a variety of points of view; but public criticism of a group of which you are a Member is, paradoxically, viewed suspiciously by those who hear it. However well-intentioned that criticism may be, it is always, without exception, self-serving in some way. Publicly critical committee Members are, therefore, doing themselves a disservice, even while trying to dissociate themselves from what they view as a bad decision.

CONCLUSION

Your role as a Member, then, while not as complex as that of the Chair, requires thought and attention. In essence, the Member facilitates the committee process. You do this both in and out of the meeting. In the meeting, itself, it is important to follow rules and to contribute to the ongoing discussion. It is also important to aid the Chair at every opportunity. Don't always leave it up to the Chair to deal with difficult Members. If you possibly can, give the Chair some relief from always having be the one to raise the hard questions. While these are certainly important parts of the Chair's job, the Chair can always use some help. Sometimes a decision can be facilitated if one or two Members fly a trial balloon, both as a way of sensing the committee position and as a vehicle for permitting the Chair to develop a compromise.

You also need to help the Chair in other ways. Sometimes, if you arrive a little early, you can assist the Chair, or a Staff person can be helped with the physical arrangements. While, again, this is not the Member's "job," the rule here is simple: we all do what needs to be done in order to ease and smooth the committee process. In some instances Members of very formal groups like boards of directors are now getting job descriptions. These help specify the kinds of things for which they are responsible and the kinds of participation expected of them. While this is a step in the right direction for such formal groups, most of us will not have this kind of instruction. The application of good sense, along the lines suggested here, is really all that is needed.

"GENERAL COMPANY"

Episode #10: "Reaching for the Top"

"Wow!" said Sally, as she and Elaine emerged from a meeting of the Building and Development Team, "that was a meeting!"

"And I'd be willing to bet that Bill's never chaired one like that before," said Elaine. "You could see that he was pleased with the way things were going; but you could also see that he didn't really understand what was happening."

"It was spectacular the way the coffeepot crowd kept stimulating the discussion and moving things along, especially when the uninitiated members kept trying to jump in and take over. But I'll tell you something—I really understand what Frank means when he says how hard it is to be a Member."

Elaine nodded in agreement. "It's particularly tough when you have to shift roles going from one meeting to the next. Just before this, I was chairing the administrative team meeting, and that's like holding rein on a herd of wild horses. Then I come to this meeting, blazing away on all cylinders, and it's all I can do to hold myself back."

"Oh, by the way, Frank wants to get together with us this

afternoon. He says he has some things to share with us about Staffer roles. After that, I suppose it'll finally be time to let Bill in on what's been going on."

"Well, you better get a handful of pins ready. I've got a hunch that Bill is going to have us handing them out like candy on Halloween."

11
The Role of the Staffer

"On errands all day I must trudge"
—W. S. Gilbert, *Thespis*

The third major collection of roles that affect meeting life and committee life belongs to the Staffer. The Staffer is a person who is paid or who has a *job assignment* related to helping a particular committee or decision-making group to carry out its purpose. "Staffer" is a term that comes from the Washington scene. We hear, for example, about committee Staffers who are hired by congressional committees to help them with a particular function. The same thing is true in other decision-making groups. Not all such groups have Staffers, and it is a confusing term for a number of reasons.

No Acceptable Name

One of these reasons is that there is really no acceptable designation within an organization for this individual. Sometimes it's an executive secretary who is asked to take a few minutes, help the committee with some of its tasks, pull together some information, and so on. At other times it's an "assistant to" an executive or someone in a relatively high position who has access to the allocation of staff service. At still other times, it is written into a job description that an individual in a particular position will assist an advisory committee or technical group in making recommendations. In some cases it's a student intern who has been assigned to an organization for a limited period of time. For all these kinds of assignments the designation Staffer is appropriate; and, at least for our discussion here, Staffer is intended to denote that individual who, through pay or job assignment, is responsible for assisting a decision-making group in carrying out its functions.

The Confusion between Staff and Staffer

A second reason for confusion lies in the fact that the "staff" of the organization, while not to be confused with the Staffer role, are frequently the very Members of the committee that we are discussing. When we think, for example, of a staff committee, we think of a committee made up of organizational members. There is no problem here. However, none of those staff members may play the Staffer role. In fact, a staff committee may have no Staffer, or individual whose job assignment it is to help them carry out their mission. The fact that there are staff members on a particular committee, or who are Members of a particular group should not be confused with the Staffer role. To clarify this point a bit more, we would emphasize that the Staffer is an assistant to the committee and not a Member of the committee. The fact that the Staffer may sit with the committee, may know its problems and difficulties intimately, does not give the Staffer membership privileges. This means that the Staffer's participation in the discussion phase of committee activity is sharply truncated. It also means that the Staffer does not have the privilege of argument. This lack of privilege to push one's own point, even though one is sitting with the committee, is a major difficulty for those of us who play the Staffer role, particularly if we have just come from earlier role performances as Chair and Member. Hence, it has to be approached very thoughtfully, and with a great deal of care.

Executive/Staffer Confusion

There's a third source of possible confusion here, which comes from the role of the Executive. In the small organization or business, or in segments of larger organizations and businesses, the Executive may form various groups to give him or her advice, to handle certain matters, or for some other particular purposes. The Executive may be the Chair of those groups. In that case, the Executive plays a dual role of Staffer and Chair, and often will seek assistance for the Staffer part of that dual responsibility.

Still, the Executive has something that other Staffers don't: the privilege of argument. In some cases, for example, at the highest levels of the organization, the Executive may be a Member of the decision-making group. Many CEOs, for example, are Members of the boards of directors of the organizations they run—and not just ex officio Members, but stock-owning, voting, inside directors. This dual role is an extremely difficult combination to pull off successfully. It's a lot like trying to conduct an orchestra from the piano; it can be done, but it's not easy. One must pay special attention to the quality of decisions that emerge when such duality is involved in the decision-making process. While role confusion and intermingling do not in every instance lead to decisional confusion and quality decrements, they certainly can; and special attention must be given to that possibility.

Many decision-making groups find it difficult to carry out all their assignments by drawing only on their own membership. The problem, of course, is time. Many of us are part of many such groups. The assignments that flow from consideration of issues within these groups are often, themselves, time-consuming and complex, to say nothing of the preparatory and meeting requirements. People with "committee talent" especially—those individuals who everyone recognizes are good to have as a part of a group and facilitate the accomplishment of committee and social purpose—tend to become overcommitted and then either burn out or withdraw. The Staffer is one solution to this problem. Once a group if formed, an individual within the organization is identified as someone (i.e., the Staffer) who can provide the kinds of assistance the group needs to carry out its mission.

STAFFER ROLES

The kinds of assistance a Staffer might provide can vary widely. Among the more typical are: the searching out of particular knowledge needed on special topics (a research function); the pulling together of material from diverse sources, both written and interview (a knowledge-synthesis function); preparation of the documentary part of the committee activity, including reports, memoranda, and minutes (a writing function); and assistance with the simple mechanics of meeting arrangements, room preparation, and so on (an administrative function). Each of these functions represents a subrole within the overall Staffer role.

The Researcher

Decision-making groups need information, as we have stressed repeatedly. Information, however, does not simply walk in and present itself to the committee. Often a great deal of work is needed to dig out the kinds of information the committee wants. Frequently, too, the kinds of things the committee needs are not immediately clear to it. Thus, the Staffer may need to pull information from a range of sources. Some of these sources are traditional ones, like the library. Others are less common, such as unpublished reports lying in the files of other organizations. It is necessary to make contact with those organizations to find out what they know about particular topics. Sometimes the committee needs to look at other organizational policies, and these must be borrowed, copied, and returned to the organization whose policies the particular group needs or wants to review. Sometimes it involves interviewing individuals about particular topics. Whatever the source of information, it is very likely that the Staffer will be going out into the community, pulling together and making available to the committee information it needs to make its decisions.

Suppose, for example, that the committee is considering staff salaries. It might want to learn what other firms and organizations are paying. It might find out what if any recommendations the national organization of the particular trade or business has made. It might want to get some information on local community conditions. If one has not already been completed, it might want to have an analysis performed of past salary practices within the organization itself. There are the types of information a Staffer probably would try to compile.

To some extent this is "gofer" work ("go for this" and "go for that"). It's necessary, however, and there's no easy way to acquire information sources other than to go after them. At various times there will be too many possibilities and too much information. In that case, in consultation with the Chair or with the committee itself, selections need to be made that are consistent with the Staffer's time. One of the disadvantages of the Researcher role is that groups always ask for (although don't necessarily want or really use) additional information. It is thus possible to have a situation in which the Staffer is running after all manner of things under conditions that do not really promise payoff in terms of work invested.

Let us emphasize here that the term "Researcher" is not meant to designate someone who develops new knowledge (such as a university researcher). Rather, we are talking about someone who pulls together information, based essentially on what is known. Every so often, however, the things that are needed won't be known. Then a small survey or exploration into new areas is very appropriate. These tend to be occasional situations, however, not really typical of the Researcher role.

The Knowledge Synthesizer

The Researcher role is one that presents information. That information, however, cannot simply be passed along whole to the committee. There are usually a number of things that need to be done to it before it can be used for decision making.

For one thing, there are often many different types of information. There may be research reports from academic or business journals and periodicals. There may be reports and documents from other organizations, businesses, government agencies, and so on. There may be interviews.

In addition to securing the information, it is the Staffer's job to synthesize that information in a state-of-the-art sense. The committee wants to know, "Given all this information, where do we stand—what do we know, where are the soft and weak spots, where is knowledge not present, and how relevant is it to the decision that we have to make?"

Pulling Information Together.   It is in this area that the Staffer can exercise a great deal of influence. The way in which information is pulled together can be particularly effective. What is included, what is excluded, what is stressed, and what is downplayed all result from shaping techniques that can guide the decision-making committee in one direction or another. It is here, of course, that the professionalism of the Staffer is most important. We do not expect that the Staffer will slant or obfuscate information in order to achieve his or her own point of view. This is part of the purpose of the Options Memo, where different options are discussed and a recommendation is made. But canons of fairness and openness do not mean that influence cannot be exercised—indeed it is. But influence should be open rather than covert.

Reconciling Ambiguities and Uncertainties.   Another type of synthesis that is contained in the procedures we have just mentioned has to do with reconciling ambiguities and uncertainties within the information sources. Anyone who has worked with information knows that on any particular topic reasonable information will vary in quality. Some will be poor and should be discarded. Other material will be of uncertain quality. The virtue of securing information from several sources lies precisely in the fact that the different sources can be used to verify each other to some extent. Still, ambiguities and uncertainties will remain; and it is up to the Staffers to point out the location and nature of such problems as the information is put together for decision-making groups.

Developing Types of Information: Historical, Scientific, Political.   There are additional concerns, as well. Not only does information differ with respect to source and quality, but it also differs with respect to type. Several types of information are crucial to high-quality decisions. One of these is historical information, or information about the precedents that govern a particular case. Usually the types of precedents we refer to here will not be legal precedents, although sometimes, of course, they will. Rather, such precedents will be in answer to such questions as: What has gone on before? What is the historical context in which we are operating in this organization at this point in time? After all, concerns and issues do not arise from nothing. They emerge from a background, from an environment of concerns; and this needs to be spelled out.

We have already touched on a second kind of information: scientific information. What are the techniques, procedures, and knowledge that have been tried and tested, and that govern our particular case? How accurate are these forecasts, estimates, and assessments? Which among them apply most directly to our case? Sometimes the Staffer will need to get professional assistance from outside the organization to come to grips firmly with such issues, but they are important bases to touch.

The last type of information is political information. What do important people (elites or bosses, for example) and others think? This information is critical. Even though the views of elites and bosses may be wrong, they represent, nevertheless, an important political element in a decisional environment. We might also need to know, depending on the issue, what particular groups think—minorities, suppliers, customers, women. It is the Staffer's job to see to it that this kind of information is available. It's time-consuming to get because it changes and is not likely to be written down the way scientific information is. Still, a few phone calls are likely to produce enough leads to follow up.

In short, the Staffer cannot simply collect and present information. The information must be collected, assessed, checked for gaps, and pulled together in some kind of usable form. A Staffer who can do this will become a cherished resource for the committee or group.

The Writer/Documentor

As the decision process flows along, and information is developed and reported, it must be put in writing. In fact, the written report is one of the most useful ways the Staffer can report the synthesized information she or he has been developing. Often, of course, we would like to rely on oral reports. Somehow this is easier, and we might even argue it on the basis of such virtues as immediacy, intimacy, and better communication. These arguments, though, are typically fraudulent. Following the rules discussed in the earlier section on meetings, the oral report does not follow the rule of Halves nor does it follow the Rule of Reports or Executive Summary. It is a problem for people to absorb information, even well-presented information, on the spot. Oral reports are useful to the extent that they are a supplement to—*never* a substitute for—a written Options Memo or Information Memo that lays out concerns, difficulties, and prospects.

The Documentor deals with keeping an adequate record of the sources consulted. This can become critical should it become necessary (as it frequently does) to go back and check a particular source. When this is necessary, inaccurate or inadequate record keeping becomes a major bane and problem, which may, in fact, have profound financial and legal (both civil and criminal) implications. "Here's the quote from old so-and-so, but I can't remember where I got it" is the kind of Staffer remark that ought to send cold chills up and down the spines of committee Members. In any kind of public document, such a quote could not be used. Neither should it ever be permitted in a private document that may affect the direction of committee decisions.

Apart from writing *to* the committee, the Staffer also writes *for* the committee. Most groups assigned to tasks need to reach some final decision or set of decisions and communicate them to appropriate authorities. The Staffer takes the lead in preparing this decision document and, in consultation with the Chair (who in turn is consulting with the membership at large), puts the final report or memorandum on paper in draft form. That done, the committee is able to go through the draft in detail, and change it, make suggestions, and produce a finalized version of the document.

The Administrator

In the Administrator role, the Staffer aids the Chair in carrying out the administrative reponsibilities of the latter. In this particular connection, the Staffer works most closely to see to it that all of the "stage manager" activities necessary for an upcoming meeting are taken care of, and that all of the clean-up and follow-through activities that result from the meeting are attended to.

Preparing the Site. As a minimum there are mechanical matters of taking care of the room, being sure that the agenda is out (following the Rule of Three Quarters), being sure before that that agenda preparation has culminated in a list of candidate items (following the Rule of Halves), and so on. This involves checking and double checking. As we mentioned in previous sections, attention to these details will not necessarily make things go right, but lack of attention to them will almost certainly make things go wrong.

Confirming the Time. A mechanical detail that often presents difficulty is setting the meeting time. For some groups, with regular meeting times, this is no trouble. For others, however, it's a very definite problem, one that may require a number of calls on the part of the Staffer before a time available to everyone is negotiated. If the group is going to meet for several sessions, those initial negotiations should probably focus on a permanent meeting time. A good technique to use here is to set up a meeting time consistent with what one believes to be the needs of the group. Then, if a particular meeting is found to be unnecessary, it can be canceled. The psychological benefits of canceling an unnecessary meeting and providing unexpected free time (as opposed to scheduling an unexpected, necessary meeting and depriving individuals of expected free time) are great. A proactive scheduling technique, therefore, is a good one.

Administrative functions extend beyond the mechanical, however. There are often follow-up tasks that need to be accomplished as the meeting comes to a close. Some of these involve getting additional information, writing new documents, and so on. Others involve touching base with particular people whom the committee views as important. There are minutes to complete and get out. There is also the beginning of the process of developing the agenda for the next meeting.

A Resource/Aide to the Chair

The Staffer serves as a resource person to consult with and help the Chair. This involves strategic considerations—sitting down with the Chair and helping him or her to think through what is happening and what is going to occur. The Aide to the Chair role encompasses much more than simply reviewing the agenda under the Rule of Halves, although that's definitely a component. The key role element here is strategic and tactical planning with respect to the items. The Chair needs someone with whom to analyze the meeting, and the Chair should and must use the Staffer for that, since it is not appropriate to use Members in that role.

There are many ways in which items can be presented, much detail and direction that must be decided upon. This is an Aide to the Chair role, much of which occurs outside the committee process. Within the meeting, the Staffer aids the Chair through the process of supporting the general thrusts of the Chair's initiatives. The Chair might suggest, for example, that more information is needed on a particular point, and the Staffer might express willingness to secure what is needed. Or, the Chair might indicate that there has been ample research done, and that more information will not aid measurably in the process of coming to a decision. We are certainly not suggesting that the Staffer is simply a yes-person; rather, that he or she plays a supportive role whenever possible. It is particularly important that the Staffer not become involved in a Member-versus-Chair situation when either responding or not responding to Members.

Because of the level of pre-meeting activity that involves Chair–Staffer consultation, the Chair and the Staffer will have an opportunity to develop strategy about the meeting, anticipating to some degree where potential difficulties might arise and having reasonable contingency plans for handling them. Pre-meeting preparation of this sort is likely to result in a process of proactivity characteristic of high-quality decisions.

In the meeting itself, the Staffer is the person who usually takes minutes. This activity falls into the Documentor role. We mention it here, as well, because the process of taking minutes can have other than documentary purposes. The Staffer, from the minutes perspective, can ask a Member for clarification of a point ("for the minutes"), which can force that Member to focus more directly on what she or he wishes to say.

Overall, then, the in-meeting activity is designed to facilitate both the process of the meeting and the strategy of the Chair for handling the meeting. The Staffer seeks to avoid second-guessing the Chair in the meeting, developing new and individualistic strategies, siding with Members against the Chair, and becoming involved in substantive arguments about material with Members.

PROBLEMS AND DIFFICULTIES IN THE STAFFER ROLE

The role of the Staffer is among the more difficult of roles because of its inherent complexities. Whenever it is necessary for you to play the role of Staffer, it is important to downplay your contribution in the meeting itself. Remember, as a Staffer, you are an *assistant* to, *not* a *Member* of, the decision-making group. It is often quite difficult to play this kind of role, particularly among friends and acquaintances. These are, after all, the people you know, and you have to adjust behavior to them. Furthermore, it is human nature for us to want to have input in the decisions that affect us and in which we are participating. Hence, simply sitting in on the meeting adds significantly to the complexity of the Staffer's role. But, keep in mind the following points.

First, the Staffer is typically taking minutes, and the minutes taker is not a good participator. This frees the Staffer to concentrate on the minutes.

Second, the Staffer is not a Member of the group in the same sense that the others are. Although the Staffer may not be as sensitive to this distinction as she or he should be, the Members of the group certainly are. They're unlikely to say anything directly, such as "Well, why are you so involved? It's our job!," but they will think it. So, the role of the Staffer is harmed by overparticipation. You would not want the maitre d' of a good, expensive restaurant to sit down at the table with you. The matire d' is a facilitator, a preparer, an organizer, a stage setter, an expeditor. We like and appreciate him in this role. For his part, the good maitre d' understands the limitations of his role, and he avoids too great a familiarity with those having dinner.

Third, the Staffer has already exerted influence through the preparation of reports, the presentation of information, and strategic discussions with the Chair. It's not a question, then, of *whether* the Staffer has influence, but the way in which that influence is expressed and the nature of the impact system that is designed. The Staffer does not participate in the give-and-take of discussion in the meeting, Rather, his influence is felt in indirect but nevertheless powerful ways.

Fourth, the very knowledge base of the Staffer is a reason for vocal temperance. In groups, people tend to defer to those who know a lot, or who seem to know a lot (as evidenced by talking a lot). Because the Staffer knows a lot, the Staffer could be a very influential person in the discussion. The problem is that Staffer participation, based heavily as it is on asserted or assumed knowledge, tends to destroy the cohesion of the group. While people will bend decisions to suit the will of the Staffer in many instances, if that will is exerted, it has a very negative effect on group cohesion. That in turn may both decrease the quality of future decisions and negatively effect the quality of current decisions because the give-and-take process—th process that is likely to spot flaws, uncover difficulties, and add strengths—does not go on as it should. In effect the group becomes, or can become, bifurcated, with group Members on one side and the Staffer on the other.

In some instances, though, the Staffer does participate. Those are worth mentioning.

Participation may occur when questions are asked about a particular report that the Staffer has been involved in, when discussion of that document is important. The Staffer may well flesh out the report, add some new bits of information that have come in since it was put together, and so on.

There is one situation in which Staffer participation may be sought, but which the wise Staffer will avoid if at all possible. It will occur when the Staffer is a professional person in his or her own right (lawyer, accountant, physician, etc.) and is called upon to render a professional opinion. This can be very hazardous for the Staffer because it is frequently a trap. Often, the kinds of areas in which professional opinion is sought are the precise ones in which a professional opinion cannot be given. If the answer were clear, it would already be known. The request for a professional opinion, therefore, is often a veiled request for a professional judgment that the interrogator feels will support his side. Under those conditions, while the Staffer may indicate what his or her professional judgment is, he or she should take particular care to indicate that it is a *judgment,* not settled opinion, and should seek to give a balanced answer. That answer should at least consider the perspectives of other Members of the group. It is all too true that on some other occasion, on another issue, Members who are not thus encompassed by the Staffer's professional judgment may well try to get revenge.

Members will respect the integrity of a Staffer role that is handled in a professional manner, where information is brought together (remember the Options Memo Technique) and the decision is left in the hands of those who have been asked to make it. As Staffers seek to insinuate themselves into this process, they become tagged. Their reputation suffers, and belief in their integrity and objectivity wanes.

A third situation in which the Staffer participates in the meeting is in the ordinary give-and-take on issues of minimal importance. The Staffer should not sit quietly then, but should join the casual banter and perhaps share a view or two. This exchange has to be carefully monitored and thought out so that it adds to the positive ambience of the meeting without becoming a sub rosa vehicle for participation.

A fourth situation of participation occurs when the Staffer is the Executive. In that case, as we have already discussed, the Staffer, as Executive, has the very definite prerogative of argument. When the Staffer is the Executive, then one expects the Staffer to participate in arguing for and standing up for particular aspects of the agenda; and it is often appropriate to do so, because the Executive may well be a full or an ex officio Member. He would have the privilege of argument and would have the privilege of preference that goes with membership.

Participation of the Staffer should be governed by good sense. It should be modest and structured in such a way as to underscore the viability of the decision-making group itself.

CONCLUSION

Without a Staff, many committees could not function. Historically, many roles, such as Executive Secretary to the Committee, Assistant to the Committee, Staff to the Committee, and so on, have been developed and used. And, they continue to a large extent to this day.

Many of us during the course of a working week, play the role of Staffer. We also play Member roles and, from time to time, Chair roles as well, as we participate in the committee and meeting processes. There are other roles, too, both formal and informal, that are a part of those processes. These we will examine in the next chapter.

"GENERAL COMPANY"

Episode #11: "M.E.E.T. the Staff"

Frank drained the last few drops out of the coffeepot into the cups of his co-conspirators. "I would have to say that our program of change has been reasonably successful."

"It sure has," said Sally. "I think we've enlisted about two thirds of the staff. Some of them aren't entirely sure what they've been enlisted into, but they're wearing their pins proudly, anyway."

"The most encouraging thing I've seen," said Elaine, "is the way people have stopped complaining about the things that they, themselves, were doing to make meetings go wrong without realizing that they were at fault. And I have to admit, before we got started on this, I was one of the biggest offenders."

"No bigger than I was," said Sally.

"Everyone is at fault when things go wrong," said Frank. "I'm probably the worst offender because I knew what to do to make them go right, but I couldn't get my own act together until you two came along."

Elaine grinned. "It's just a matter of having the right staff."

Sally also smiled. "And having them behave like staff. I'll tell you something. The idea that you have to play a role as a Staffer that's different from the role you play as a Member or as a Chair was completely new to me."

"It's completely new to most people," said Frank, "but you two have made yourselves great role models for the rest of the people at Omnibus."

"We've had a good teacher," said Sally.

"Well, class, now we come to the hardest part of this course."

"And that is?" Elaine asked.

"Telling Bill what's been going on. Let's go."

12
The Role Repertoire

"How shall I play this part?"
—W. S. Gilbert, *The Grand Duke*

In this section we have talked about three roles specifically: the Chair, the Member, and the Staffer. These are the major, formal "assigned" roles that one finds in the decision-making group. They are, perhaps, the central or focal roles, but they're not the only ones, and in this chapter we want to speak about some other formal roles—Vice President, Secretary, and so forth—and the less formal roles that are either assigned to or taken on by some individuals, such as Enabler, Process Leader, Scapegoat, Task Leader, and so on. Finally, and perhaps most important, it's necessary to stress the need for role flexibility, or to recognize the need to switch from role to role—both on an intervening basis, as one switches from meeting to meeting and from group to group, and also on an intervening basis as the dynamic process of group activities evolves and changes.

OTHER FORMAL ROLES

In many groups there are some other formal role assignments that are given to people, in addition to those discussed in the preceding three chapters. These can range from officerships within the context of boards of directors to Chairships and headships of various subcommittees, both of the board and within the context of the organization.

Associate Head (Vice Chair)

This designation can be used to denote a Vice Chair or deputy head of any decision-making group. It is an important role, and, typically, that individual fills in when the Chair is absent; but that is the least of the responsibilities an associate head has. An associate can share with the Chair the responsibility for carrying out the rules and purposes of the committee or group in question. Sometimes Chairship, because of its manifold duties, especially with respect to administration and generalized task assignments of that sort, becomes quite onerous. Here an associate or deputy can be of great service. Some deputies take over the job of working with the Staffer in meeting planning and preparation. Others will alternate this role with the Chair. Too, deputies sometimes take on some parts of the committee assignment as their special responsibility and work. This is especially helpful when the topical areas covered by a particular decision-making group are widely varied and substantively disparate.

On a less formal basis, a deputy or associate will assist the Chair in a meeting itself, often sharing with the Chair responsibilities for tempering the overparticipator and enhancing the role of underparticipator. As a semiofficial/semimember, the associate is in a good position to take some of the risks from the Chair, and to move things by suggestion or motion to a conclusion.

Often, the associate will seek to complement the Chair. If the Chair feels the need to stress process and involvement in a particular meeting, the associate may complement that through emphasis on task accomplishment. If, on the other hand, the Chair focuses upon task accomplishment, a complementary role involving process emphasis might be appropriate.

It is very important for the associate to try to relate and adjust to the Chair's style and wishes. It is especially important to avoid the appearance and the reality of competing with the Chair for the allegiance of committee Members.

The associate will also spend some time talking with the Chair to get a feel for what the Chair's interest will be, and what his or her effort is likely to encompass. And, on some occasions the associate can represent the Chair and the committee at external functions, though not so often as to appear to have become the de facto Chair.

Secretary

For civic and other important boards, a Secretary will be elected or appointed. It's often thought that the job of the Secretary is to take minutes. Historically, this was true of all secretaries; and to some extent, if there is no staff assistance, it is still appropriate for the Secretary to undertake this task. Yet, it is not really advisable (and in most instances is not really appropriate) for the Secretary to be the actual, physical minutes taker. The reason for this, of course, is that the person who takes minutes can't participate very well in a meeting. Hence, to be asked to take minutes is to have an ambiguous role with respect to participation. Generally, it is better to let the Staffer take minutes so the Secretary can serve in a sort of archivist capacity, reviewing past minutes and adding to the agenda those items that are contained in the minutes and need to be dealt with again. In particular, Secretaries should be able to comment upon historical or past practice as represented in the minutes with respect to particular forthcoming issues. "Have we ever done this before?" and "Have we ever had this kind of problem before?" are questions that the Secretary should be able to answer with relevant information and documents from the previous consideration.

Treasurer

Civic boards will have a Treasurer, an individual who oversees the financial matters of the organization and often countersigns its checks, particularly in small, nonprofit organizations. In those cases it is useful to have the Treasurer bonded. This should be done as a matter of established policy. Such a policy avoids hurt feelings or the suspicion of dishonesty on the part of anyone. Treasurers, like other officials in the organization who make reports, need to get over the idea that they should appear on the agenda as a single item. Their training should focus upon breaking their reports into decisional, discussion, and informational items. That will enable a more cogent handling of the topics they generate, based upon the nature of the topic, and will correspond to following the Rule of the Agenda Bell.

All too often, Treasurers' views of their role are quite limited. The Treasurer is viewed as the safeguard of money and a tightfisted curmudgeon who won't let funds drain out of the organization. Certainly, a careful review of expenditure patterns and reporting on them is appropriate to the Treasurer role. However, Treasurers also have the responsibility of bringing the organization up to organizational snuff, with respect to new and innovative ways to handle financial matters. Thus, the Treasurer should be an individual conversant with, and broadly knowledgeable about, fiscal techniques and methods and their application, particularly in the case of civic boards and voluntary organizations. These qualifications are more likely to be a problem in such organizations, since the Treasurers in corporate organizations tend to be paid and have that role as a fulltime job.

Subcommittee Chairs

Often a group will establish a subcommittee, asking one of its Members, as the Subcommittee Chair, to look into a particular area, and, alone or with the assistance of others, to bring back a report that the organization can use to discuss a problem under consideration. This is grist for the organization mill, and such assignments should be taken seriously. The key element, of course, is to approach the matter from an information-seeking and recommending posture. It really wouldn't be appropriate for a subgroup of the organization, chaired by a board member, to come up with recommendations so tight and so complete that they could not be challenged by other Members of the group. Indeed, "challenged" is not even an appropriate word here. "Considered," "combined," "reshaped" are all words that talk more about the kind of report and posture that is desired. Recall that our tendency to think stereotypically seems to be enhanced when we have very few options to choose from. Hence, it is up to the Subcommittee Chair to use the Options Memo Technique to try to broaden the range of subcommittee possibilities that are actually brought to the whole committee.

Guest

The preceding are only a sampling of other formal roles that one may play in the committee process. We cannot leave this discussion without considering one last, important role: Guest. One may play the role of Guest as a result of having been invited to sit in, either on the basis of membership on another related committee or out of interest and concern. Often, as a matter of deference, Chairs will ask if the Guest has anything to add. This offer should almost always be graciously declined except to provide a little informational perspective from the visitor's own organization. It's altogether too easy to slip into the role of Member. Even though the group invites Guests to do it, they resent it if someone actually takes advantage of the invitation.

The Guest may be invited only for one particular part of the meeting. When this is the case, it should be understood in advance if possible. In the interests of both courtesy and efficiency, Guests should be told whether they are invited to stay for the whole meeting or only until some particular presentation is made. Many embarrassing incidents could be avoided if this type of information were clarified. Also, Guests should seek to learn in advance the amount of time that they are expected to devote to their appearance if their invitation is in respect to a particular item or a presentation of a particular item. All too often great mistakes are made in this regard, and people go on much too long, or, less frequently but not unheard of, are simply not ready with the kind of detail that it was expected they would have.

In the well-run group, these kinds of things will be taken care of at the initiative of the Chair. Since most groups are not run well, it is certainly better for Guests to take it upon themselves to determine their situation.

INFORMAL ROLES

There are a number of informal roles that one can undertake or be assigned. These require careful attention at some points because they can become sex-linked and be a way of communicating lower status especially. For example, there seems to be an overall tendency to ask women to take the minutes and to handle any small amounts of food preparation or housekeeping chores that may be involved. While these kinds of stereotypic assignments should not be made, they all too frequently are. It is up to the officers, the heads of committees, and the Members of the group to resist these kinds of routine and traditional divisions of labor.

Task Leader

One of the more important informal roles one should know about is that of Task Leader. The Task Leader takes it upon him- or herself to remind the group continually that there is work to be done, and keeps persuading, pushing, and encouraging the group to accomplish the tasks that it has before it. Such an individual is a real asset to the group, provided the role is not overdone. If it is overdone, it can become counterproductive, and the Task Leader's own drive to action becomes instead a signal for delay and inaction on the part of the group.

Often the Task Leader needs to undertake some external tasks that will help accomplish what is needed. This person, though, needs to be sensitive to the fact that helpful individuals tend to be resented over time. Perhaps, one should say "especially helpful" individuals. Hence, the Task Leader needs to recognize that he or she does not own the group or the group's destiny. Pressures to accomplish more and to do so more efficiently and more effectively are always in order, but in the final analysis it is really up to the group to decide whether it wants that kind of accomplishment to occur.

Process Leader

The Process Leader is the one who seeks to provide involvement, soothes ruffled feelings, tells jokes and other tension-breaking stories at crucial times, acts as a recognizer and supporter of an underdog on a particular issue, and in general tries to help facilitate the social and emotional climate of the group. These things are often done in connection with Task Leaders. Process is crucial. Without the bonding and blending created by process leadership, tasks could not be accomplished.[1]

When groups go on for a while, Members may get assigned to particular informal roles, based upon the overall group assessment of the nature and quality of their contribution. Terms such as "dummy ," "nit picker," and "smart ass" are often used to describe an individual's reputation within the group context. Almost any aspect of committee content that one stresses all the time will, or is likely to, result in some kind of role assignment, even if the individual doesn't want it. Minorities, women, and others who have symbolic roles in the larger society are often used in this capacity within the decision-making group. Somebody may turn to a black Member and ask, "Jim, what do the blacks think about this?"; or ask a woman member, "Sally, what do the women think about that?"; or ask, "Saul, what is the Jewish community's view?"—and so on. It's difficult to free

[1] Still, task accomplishment is not always the reason for a group's existence. Sometimes, paradoxically, the real purpose of groups is process achievement. Tasks are merely the formal and secondary vehicle to that end. We seem to need the charade of task accomplishment because we find it difficult to get together for the simple purpose of improving group communication and cohesion. This is unlikely to be well regarded in many circles. To get around that difficulty we may invent tasks or undertake tasks of only marginal importance in order to permit people to do what they would like and need to do. Under such conditions, excessive task leadership is not only fruitless, it is counterproductive, since only a certain amount of task accomplishment aids process improvement point for point. Too much task accomplishment in these circumstances can tear at the fabric of group cohesion, group meaning, and group sensibilities.

ourselves from this kind of stereotyping. It is tough enough to do even when we are of a mind to do it. If we unknowingly fall into these roles or assume them, it becomes even more difficult.

THE ROLE REPERTOIRE

Perhaps the best cure for some of the improper "role fixations" is a definite attempt to develop a varied and flexible role repertoire. We need to keep in mind that, if you are good at anything, people will keep after you to perform it until you finally fail. At that point they will cluck and say, "Well, he wasn't quite as good as he thought." Whatever else competence breeds, some resentment is likely to result. The ability to change roles can soften this resentment and deflect the routine assignments of roles to oneself.

A point that needs special emphasis here is that it is important for the individual to take responsibility for role flexibility. Sometimes, for example, assume a Task Leadership position; at others, a Process Leadership role is more important. Move around from role to role. Try to avoid becoming typecast in one particular role within the organization. Sometimes talk a lot. Other times talk a little. Not only will this make it more interesting for you, but it will prevent the stereotyping of you and your qualities that would lead to your being disregarded and not fully attended to.

The role repertoire, then, involves the deliberate development of a role ensemble that includes performance capabilities in Chair, Member, and Staff roles as well as the other formal and informal roles to which one aspires. Partly, the role you play in any given meeting or in any given group depends upon what others are doing, just as individuals in a musical ensemble might shift their performance depending upon who shows up and what capabilities those present have. In a meeting you do the same.

But it's not just a question of who shows up. Meetings have their own dynamics, and sometimes they take off in a way that demands some Task Leadership; at other times, Process Leadership is required. It's essential, therefore, not only to have the inherent role knowledge and role flexibility needed, but to develop the ability to shift roles as the occasion demands. Certainly, in the course of a day, many of us will play many different roles. The crucial aspect here, and the one to keep constantly in mind, is that it is necessary to adjust the roles (as Goffman suggested) to the particular "play" we are in. Not only will such adjustment, role shifting, and flexibility help in the task and process accomplishment of particular groups we happen to be in at the moment, but it will help us, as individuals, to avoid becoming typecast, being identified as those who "always" perform in specific ways. Role lock-in, or role fixation, in which a particular individual always "gets to" or "does" play a particular role, certainly has its roots in social expectations and conventions. To a degree, though, the individual contributes to it. The idea is not to blame the victim. Instead, look for ways in which, through the presentation of a varied role posture, you can give diverse, rather than constant, signals about what you can do. Women, for example, because of the historical propensity of men to expect process performance, should make a point of taking task roles from time to time. Men should deliberately seek process opportunities. People should talk a lot, then a little. You will not only get a wide range of role experience here, but you will also demonstrate that you have different competencies.

CONCLUSION

The committee, the meeting, has often been thought of as a sort of roleless lump in which people get together without much idea of what they are going to do and with expectations that things go downhill from there. It needn't be this way. Attention to the rather wide range of roles that are available—formal and informal—can materially improve the process of the group and the quality of decision making. Good role performance within the group adds to quality; diverse role performance among group members adds luster and class to them, both individually and collectively.

"GENERAL COMPANY"

Episode #12: "Finale—It's Over"

Bill fingered the small white button with the black coffeepot that Sally had just pinned on his lapel. "So *that's* what this has been all about. I'm really a bit relieved. I had visions of walking in here one day and finding that my desk had been moved to the basement. Well, you went about it the long way, but I've got to admit you proved your point."

"We really didn't have much choice," Elaine said. "You were pretty negative about meetings."

"That's true. I always thought they were something like the common cold, something that had to be endured but that no one could really do anything about."

"And if we had come to you in the beginning with our plan," said Frank, "you would have told us that it wasn't worth much investment of organizational time."

"Guilty, as charged," said Bill.

"And we didn't really invest all that much time," said Sally. "We got together every few days during coffee breaks or after work. And we shared information with the other people in the M.E.E.T. conspiracy in the normal course of the work day, after we swore them to secrecy, of course."

"I have to admit, there's been a lot of interest. The staff has viewed it as a kind of game, and a good many of them have started to play that game very well. Most of our meetings have shown marked improvement. What's the next step?"

"We've talked about that," said Frank. "We think M.E.E.T. should become a regular part of our business operations at Omnibus. We need an ongoing program of staff training on meeting performance. We could even make part of the staff development package special training in Chairship, Membership, and Staffship so that our people will have at least a rudimentary idea of appropriate role performance. We don't want to surround the whole thing with bureaucracy, at least to the point where it becomes a pain in the neck. What we have in mind is to give our people a little bit of useful knowledge and let them take it from there.''

"And once we get the central office moving," said Sally, "we can begin to send some of these ideas out to our field offices."

"And the material we've put together," said Elaine, "has much wider applicability than just our company. A good many of us are on boards and committees of civic and church and social organizations."

"I've got an immediate application for it," said Bill. "I've been asked to be on the national board of a charitable organization my church runs. They've been having a lot of communication and organizational difficulties. When they called me, they said they thought they needed business techniques to help them. I think, now, I have something really useful to share with them."

"Then are we to take it that you approve of the M.E.E.T. conspiracy?" Frank asked

"Wholeheartedly," said Bill.

"Well, then," said Elaine, "there is a certain formality."

A suspicious look crept across Bill's face. "I see. I suppose I have to sign some sort of articles of conspiracy."

"No," said Sally, "but you do have to buy us all a doughnut."

PART IV. SPECIAL MEETINGS CONCERNS

The material covered thus far has dealt with why things go wrong, and rules and roles to make things go right. We have presented general formulations that are applicable to a wide range of settings, and that is as it should be. There ought to be some principles that can be followed whether the meeting is being held here or there, in the executive suite or in the mail room.

It has been our experience in using these materials that they are, indeed, broadly applicable. At the same time, as one gets into more specific types of decision-making groups, the need for additional, more specific information with respect to those groups increases. Consider, for example, the staff meeting, that bete noire of our organizational life that seems so necessary at the same time that it seems so useless. Consider, too, the advisory committee we are so often asked to serve on. Sometimes we'll be asked to help out on an advisory committee—either technical or general in nature—to other groups, such as professional, civic, or business organizations. There is also the civic board, which allows us to fulfill a civic duty.

There is a vast range in the types of groups that are involved in decision making. It is not possible to cover them all, but we can touch on a few.

A related point, however, is that decision-making groups are rarely of a single type. Often, a particular group, such as a staff group, might cycle through a range of functions—decision-making, advisory, search, and so on—even in the course of a single relatively brief period. This requires not only a facility within the individual role repertoire—we've already discussed that—but it implies, indeed requires, a facility within the group itself.

We have selected three groups to discuss in detail:

1. The Staff Meeting
2. The Advisory Committee
3. The Civic Board

As before, the information is drawn from discussions with a wide range of individual participants, in dozens of different types of decision-making groups, and represents a distillation of their wisdom and perspectives.

13
The Staff Meeting

"And lend me all your aid."
—W. S. Gilbert, *The Sorcerer*

Most of us do not think of a Staff Meeting as a "committee" or a decision-making group at all. Instead, we tend to regard it as a group of people who know each other, who get together to . . . to . . . *to do what?* That turns out to be one of the most serious problems of the Staff Meeting. All too often it's extremely unclear why people are getting together. All too often the perception is, "We get together every week because we always get together every week." One of the great problems of Staff Meetings, therefore, is to specify the purpose for which a meeting is being held.

"Ah," the argument goes, "but there are many purposes for the Staff Meeting." No question about it, that's very likely to be the case. Sometimes issues come up for decision. Sometimes issues come up for discussion. Sometimes information is presented. Those are the same three types of processes that occur in any group. The staff group, then, is really not so different, at least in the things that it does. What *is* different is the degree of informality and lack of care with which we create this particular kind of gathering.

FUNDAMENTAL PROBLEMS

The lack of clarity that characterizes Staff Meetings stems in part from the familiarity of the participants. Time and again people have told us: "We don't need to worry about all these rules within the Staff Meeting. We know all these people. They are our friends. We work with them every day. This kind of stuff is too formal."

Unfortunately, they're right about part of what they believe but wrong about the implied conclusion. That implied conclusion goes something like this: "Since I know these people and work with them on a daily basis, I can handle the kinds of things that need to be handled when we get together; elaborate preparations—or any preparations at all—are not necessary; besides, I'd probably feel embarrassed about this 'formality' with people I know well.

The difficulty in this line of thinking stems from the fact that quality decisions have relatively little to do with whether the decision makers know each other well or not. It's true that, if the participants know one another well, there is likely to be greater cohesion. This *may* effect some marginal improvement with respect to the decision. Basically, however, what is needed is information and a process or structure that permits that information to be systematically and usefully considered. The fact that people know each other, while building a bit of cohesion, tends to work against the structuring of information flow for maximum utility at key meeting points. In addition, it may engender an informal and unsystematic process of issue consideration that actually harms the quality of the decision.

There's a third point to be considered, as well. When we know people and deal with them on a daily basis, there are always many more issues latent within the group than are currently on the table. While these "hidden agendas" are always present, they tend to be more likely in groups of people who work with each other on a daily basis. The potential for issue confusion and confounding, as a result, is inordinately high.

Hidden agendas cannot be removed. Often, people speak of

them as if they were a case of bad tonsils that could be surgically removed by a skillful Chair. Like so many of our beliefs about the group decision-making process, this fantasy draws its energy more from the wishes of people than from the reality of events. Thus it is that rules and procedures agreed upon by the group are even more important. Indeed, as emotions run higher, as confounding conditions flourish, the importance of procedure increases.

APPLYING THE RULES

Among the most important rules for Staff Meetings to follow are the Rule of Halves and, in particular, the division of items into informational, decisional, and discussion categories. It's not possible to characterize the staff group entirely as an information-receiving, decision-making, or discussion group. All three purposes (plus more because there are some social and interactional purposes, as well) usually are served at each meeting. Great care must be taken, therefore, to focus in advance on the nature of each issue. In that way the problem is solved. It's not necessary to characterize the group as any particular type. Rather, each issue is focused upon within the context of a predefined category. Decision issues are thus discussed and decided, whereas discussion issues are examined and not decided. Confusion between the two is minimized. Information issues are also clearly labeled.

This simple procedure can, itself, create some problems that should be mentioned because Executives and others on the staff may seek to use a finessing procedure with respect to somewhat controversial issues. The finesse occurs when someone (the boss or in some circumstances a committee Member) seeks to "report" for "information" an issue which that individual secretly suspects should have been decided upon by the group. In effect, that person is saying: "I'm going to float this and announce it as information. If there's a big stink, I'll have to reconsider; but, since I don't want to reconsider, I'll wait to see what the reaction is.'' It is less likely that this can occur if items are clearly labeled.

The process of issue disaggregating within the Rule of Halves is also appropriate here, and particularly at this point in our discussion. All too frequently, Staff Meetings are simply litanies of announcements. Individuals who attend such meetings often wonder (with excellent cause) whether their attendance was required—whether, indeed, the meeting was really necessary. Partly because of the finesse technique, bosses are more inclined than staff to think that the meetings are necessary. On the other hand, in setting procedures up this way, bosses are systematically excluding good input from staff. If one takes the Rule of Halves seriously, then it's always possible to look carefully at an informational item and extract from it some decisional elements. Items tend not to be entirely for decision, discussion, or information. In fact, it is very likely that an item will contain some element of each. Because we inappropriately lump them together, we don't make it clear which part is which. For this reason it's useful to separate the items—particularly the informational ones—so that the remaining decision points, even though they may not be large ones, can be specifically identified and dealt with.

These considerations mean that the Rule of the Agenda Bell may need to be modified somewhat for the Staff Meeting because one issue may contain elements that might fit into modest, moderate, and most difficult item categories or might fit, as well, into the discussion category. The modification appropriate here is to schedule the item under the Rule of the Agenda Bell based upon a "predominant characterization" rule. The way that you might characterize an item *predominantly* is the key to locating it within the meeting agenda. If it is predominantly a discussion item, it should be treated as such even though it may have some decisional components.

A second modification has to do with information items that are known to be controversial. If an announcement is reasonably certain to cause discussion and negative comments, then it should be treated as a discussion item, not an information item.

This will locate it in the Item Six category and mean that it is placed in a part of the agenda where there is opportunity to spend the time needed for discussion. Careful labeling of the item on the agenda, however, is important. In order to forestall the staff's potential for misconstruing it as still up for discussion, careful construction includes noting which part is the information part and what remaining elements, if any, are up for discussion.

ROLE CONFUSION

Roles become a confusing factor here, as well. The boss of the unit is usually Chair of the Staff Meeting and principal agenda scheduler and crafter. The boss's own work schedule may not permit her or him to spend as much time doing the agenda workup as might be required. Such an individual, therefore, would be wise to ask another member of the staff to serve as Staffer for a period of time, long enough to permit some skill to develop.

The Staffer role here can be tough, especially if one is working with an Executive who has a penchant for slapping a few things down to "see which way the wind is blowing." It's equally difficult with the Executive who likes to wait until everyone gets to the meeting to see what they want to talk about.

A related difficulty involving the boss has to do with the expression of disagreement or opposition within the Staff Meeting. There is potential for a conflict that is not easy to resolve. On the one hand, the object is to get ideas from other people. On the other, there is a hierarchy of authority that, for purposes of the Staff Meeting, starts with the boss. Opposition to a particular proposal in the meeting can have ramifications that extend way beyond the meeting. It may not be possible to solve this problem totally, but everyone will breathe a lot easier if an overall clarification is made with respect to how a particular boss chooses to use the Staff Meeting.

Some bosses like to use the Staff Meeting as an advisory committee. This is certainly a legitimate use. Issues come up; staff decide which way they, as staff, would like to go; and in effect (though it is often unexpressed—and herein lies the problem) the boss either accepts or rejects this input and makes an independent decision based on it and whatever other input is available. This way of proceeding is acceptable as long as everybody understands that the boss is really making two decisions: to consider or not to consider the group's input and *then* the independent decision itself. Other bosses like to get involved with the group, and make the decision within the group context, so that whatever decision is then made carries the day. The same type of clarification needs to be made, however. As long as the staff group knows what its general posture is supposed to be, it can probably adjust and adapt to it. A lack of understanding about the role and position the staff will play in the meeting is unsettling and hinders productivity and involvement.

The Five P System

The systematic consideration of issues is important. Such systematic consideration is always crucial, but in the Staff Meeting, where intimacies run high and knowledge of each other is well developed, attention to systematic procedures for considering issues is especially critical. In such a case the Five P System might be useful. The system has the following components:

1. Problem formulation
2. Policy proposals
3. Policy ratification
4. Planning
5. Program

The first two items are predecisional steps that lead up to the actual policy decision itself. The fourth item involves designing the implementation plans implied by the policy ratified in step three. Step five is the actual carrying out of those plans. Problems and difficulties may occur at any phase and between phases. Hence, it is helpful to use this five-step decisional structure in the Staff Meeting as a way to focus upon where one is in the discussion itself. Typical Staff Meeting discussions range back and forth over the whole lot of elements. The difficulty is that it is problematic to discuss planning when a policy decision has not been made. It is difficult to discuss what policy should be selected when options are not available. And, it is probably foolish to discuss options when the problem has been only ethereally specified.

The use of such a decisional guideline or set of process steps is even more important because of two elements that are characteristic of Staff Meetings: (1) the merger of formal and informal power structures, and (2) the merger of various organizational sectors with differential responsibility for different organizational dimensions.

As we are all aware, the formal and informal power structures do not always fit together nicely. There are individuals who have formal positions of authority and power, but who, for whatever reasons, choose not to exercise it. There are other people with less well-defined formal positions who wield a great deal of influence. It is typically in the Staff Meeting that a number of these different influence components come together. Thus the possibility of friction is reasonably high, but a relatively well-ordered discussion framework will facilitate the accomplishment of high-quality decision making.

A second related but distinct problem concerns the assembly of different sectors of the organization—finance, personnel, engineering, safety, operations, and so on. Each of these subunits within the organization typically works within itself and may not necessarily know a great deal about or have contact with other units. The Staff Meeting provides a place where problems are assessed, options considered, decisions made, plans laid out, and programs designed. Not only do policies and programs have an impact on these departments (and, hence, their wish to participate), but also in a number of instances their cooperation will be required for implementation of any decision made. Once again, therefore, the likelihood of conflict among the different sectors of the organization can be mitigated in part by use of standardized discussion and decision processing techniques.

The need for such techniques, as discussed elsewhere in this book and in this chapter, is even higher because the sectors of the organization are likely to have their own culture, their own way of doing things. As a result, we can expect not only structural clashes but clashes of belief and style as well.

CONCLUSION

The Staff Meeting, then, is one of the places where a lot of work can be done or a lot of time can be wasted. The scheduling of agendas for Staff Meetings, with a careful following of the Rule of Halves and an assembling of the information and people required to handle issues that are scheduled, will facilitate not only the quality of decisions, but the interest that meeting holds for potential participants. As they show up more and are more alert, decision quality will be further enhanced.

14

The Advisory Committee

It would be unusual for an executive if she or he were not asked at some time to join an Advisory Committee. Yet, there is a great deal of confusion and uncertainty about what Advisory Committees actually are, what they do, and what they should do. There is also relatively little comprehension of some basic rules regarding their operation. In this chapter we hope to clarify the purpose and mission of the Advisory Committee and lay out a few techniques that will help in its operation.

THE NATURE OF THE ADVISORY COMMITTEE

The Advisory Committee is designed, of course, to give advice. As simple as that statement sounds, it is very hard to put into practice. People like to make decisions; they do not like to think that their decisions are being given to someone else who might reject them. It's the job of the Advisory Committee to consider a problem and recommend a solution or a range of solutions for it. Members of the committee, the Chair, and any Staffers who are assigned to it must work very hard to see that this central aspect of the committee's mission is understood. The "decision" made by the Advisory Committee is a decision on a piece of advice.

The informal power of Advisory Committees runs the gamut. Some are so influential that their advice is tantamount to a decision. Others have so little influence that it doesn't make any difference what they say. Most Advisory Committees, however, are, relatively speaking, in the middle. They have some influence but not as much as they would like or as much, often, as they think they need to accomplish their task. It is also true that many Advisory Committees relate to an executive decision maker—often a very prestigious individual. Indeed, interaction with prestigious persons is one of the key elements that attracts people to Advisory Committees; but that very fact can cause problems.

Advisory Committees may be technical or general in nature. In the case of the Technical Advisory Committee, it is usual that the Members are highly qualified in some small area. They serve as a real or quasi panel of experts in particular areas. In the General Advisory Committee, individuals of strength, prestige, and general competence usually review broad-gauge matters of a strategic rather than a technical or tactical nature and try to chart on an advice-giving basis longer-term implications and policy for the organization in question.

FUNCTIONAL PROBLEMS

There are several problems that the Advisory Committee needs to be aware of and act to circumvent. One has already been mentioned: lack of clarity about mission and roles. It should be established very early that the purpose of the Advisory Committee is to give advice. That is a legitimate function, and it should be presented in that way. Often, the Chairs of Advisory Committee say, "We are only giving advice," using a variety of words such as "only," "merely," "just," and so on, that downplay and implicitly criticize the role of the Advisory Committee Member and rob it of dignity.

A second thing that should be established early is that advice should be in writing. All too often the Advisory Committee follows a scenario that goes something like this:

> The committee was sitting around when the president of Multi-Versic Multi-Phasic walked in. He served as a sort of Chair/Recipient-of-Advice. It was not really clear to anyone whether this was a staff meeting, an advisory committee meeting, or what. He tossed a few things out that were on his mind, and people responded to them. After an hour of generalized B.S., he got up, thanked everybody profusely and left. When he got back to his office, he talked with his assistant.
> "Those advisory committee meetings drive me crazy," he said. "All we do is shoot the breeze."

Communicating in writing not only avoids the propensity for drop-of-the-lip discussion, but it also provides a record for others and for the committee archives of the kinds of activities the committee undertook, the kinds of topics they considered, and the advice they gave. Amazing at it seems, committees will often forget what advice they gave. A written piece of advice also is something that can be reviewed carefully by the committee and can carry the committee's stamp. It's unlikely that the Advisory Committee will always agree on a piece of advice, but the advisee needs to know what the overall view was and what the minority view was. This is very near to impossible if the meetings are usually gossip sessions with individuals talking to one another and to the advisee. Written advice also provides material for the Decision Audit/Decision Autopsy, which we discussed earlier.

It is also useful for the advisee not to be Chair of his or her own Advisory Committee. There are a couple of reasons for this. First, of course, it is difficult to receive advice while Chairing a group that may want to advise against something that you, as Chair, want to do. Since individuals are less likely to be negative with you in the Chair seat as Executive, then you are failing to achieve the very purpose for which the Advisory Committee was created. Thus, it is useful for Advisory Committees to have a regular Chair drawn from the committee and for the advisee to come and go.

THE SPLIT AGENDA TECHNIQUE

One thing that happens with Advisory Committees, particularly when the advisee is prestigious, is that the advisee's presence tends to make it more difficult for other work to be accomplished. An inordinate amount of attention and energy tends to be given to the advisee. Under such conditions, it is unlikely that productive work in the form of high-quality decision making will be accomplished. Therefore, it is useful for Advisory Committees to meet for some periods of time without the advisee. We recommend that this be done at every other meeting. If holding a meeting alone is not possible, then schedule an hour or two during the meeting, itself, to be free to handle the business of the day without the presence of the advisee. That business can be prepared, of course, according to the rules we have suggested, since there is no difference between making a decision about advice and making any other kind of decision. If possible, schedule the advisee to come during the second part of the meeting. This will increase the likelihood that the committee will get some business done before the potential disruption of the advisee's visit.

As a practical matter, the very presence of the advisee violates some of the things we have been talking about. Such advisees are likely to bring up things that are just fresh on their minds, and the kinds of preparation and organization that we have stressed are less likely to occur. Why bother?

In this case there is reason to bother. It is useful for advisees to have a chance to chat informally with Members of Advisory Committees. In a way, these can be viewed as informal discussion type sessions. It is a mistake to believe that high-quality decisions will come out of such sessions, at least on a regular basis. They provide a way, however, for individuals to find out something about the boss's thinking. They also let the boss move from the pre-problem to the problem stage, at least, or move further along the Five P train.

CONCLUSION

Advisory Committees are among the most problematic groups because of lack of certainty about their function and because of role confusion. If these uncertainties can be clarified, if the Split Agenda Technique can be used, and if advice can be given in writing, a number of their most serious problems can be resolved.

15
Civic Boards of Directors

"To help unhappy commoners and add to their enjoyment,
Affords a man of noble rank congenial employment."
—W. S. Gilbert, *The Gondoliers*

Many of us in the course of our professional lives serve on Civic Boards. They could be for charitable organizations, such as local or national March of Dimes or United Way groups; they could be for libraries, civic symphonies, and so on. They can often be problematic for Members; and the principles embodied in the rules and roles discussed here do apply to them.[1] There are a number of unique features to Civic Boards, however, that bear mention. These tend to be in the area of substantive responsibility, for care must be taken to assure that the charges and expectations that surround membership are carried out.

There are six main areas of responsibility that the Civic Board needs to take into consideration:

1. Legal
2. Trusteeship of civic purpose
3. Decision making
4. Establishing the proper Board organization

[1] Whereas the emphasis of this chapter is upon Civic Boards, the material has relevance for all boards of directors because the requisites of "boardship" are not substantially different for the "profits" and the "nonprofits."

5. Selection and evaluation of the Executive
6. Training and development

LEGAL

It used to be that one did not have to do right while doing good. If a group had a public or social purpose, or if it were a nonprofit organization of some kind, that would be sufficient to protect Board Members and, perhaps, staff, too, from being sued. In today's age of accountability, that is no longer the case. William Zelman (1977) has written about the kinds of legal responsibilities the Board Member has. It is, of course, important that you check the nonprofit codes in your state. (California, for example, has recently revised these codes.)

Essentially, it is important that one be diligent in attending to the duties of Civic Board membership. Diligence is often demonstrated by attendance at meetings and fulfillment of other statutory obligations.

Another term, a bit looser in its interpretation, is prudence. Civic Board Members are required to show prudence in the handling of the affairs of the corporation. Generally, this means that they have to show that they took as much care as a reasonable individual would have taken in the handling of his or her own affairs. Casual decision making and lack of appropriate procedures and safeguards are potential sources of trouble for Civic Board Members.

Conflict of interest must be given special consideration. While it usually is not required that conflict of interest be absent, it usually is required that conflict of interest be declared. Thus, if an individual wishes to do business as a Member of a Civic Board with a firm in which he or she is otherwise involved, that link must be made public, and that disclosure must appear in the minutes.

Concern about potential liabilities, arising from a citizen's or client's perception of dereliction of duty, has led to the development of directors' insurance. Directors of civic and other nonprofit organizations might want to consider this insurance.

TRUSTEES OF CIVIC PURPOSE

Legal reponsibilities are the minimal ones; that is, organizations are required, as are Directors, to meet basic standards of compliance. These details, however, do not speak to the larger issue. Usually Civic Boards can be thought of as trustees of some rather ambiguous and ill-defined civic purpose. The fact that there is ambiguity and lack of precise definition here should not be taken as anything other than par for the course. Indeed, many business firms suffer from similar ambiguities. In his book *Megatrends,* John Naisbett asks business firms to consider the question of "what business they're in." If they are not able to respond adequately, he suggests a second question: "What business would it be useful for you to think of yourself as being in?" Variations of these questions can be addressed to civic organizations. The first would go something like this: "For what purposes are we trustee?" If that question cannot be answered, then a larger, more encompassing question needs to be asked: "For what purposes would it be useful for us to consider ourselves to be the trustee?"

Most typically, as within business firms, purposes are defined for a relatively fixed period of time. For example, a five- or six-year plan is probably long enough. Multi-year plans can be renewed, if at the end of that time it seems wise to continue in that direction; or they can be changed and adjusted if the environment makes that appropriate. This is something that requires constant thought and review, however. Not only must the purposes, themselves, be considered and reconsidered—and that's a very important task—but the programmatic and structural ways in which those purposes are made reality also need to be assessed. Sometimes the purposes continue to be fine, but substantial questions might be raised about the way in which they are being put into operation. At other times, the operation may suggest that fresh sets of purposes need to be developed.

The whole point here for the Civic Board is to start from the notion that there is a civic trusteeship role. The lack of specific definition makes that role more complex and difficult. Still, efforts need to be made to find out what the community thinks and to incorporate those views into the operation of the organization.

DECISION MAKERS

In today's Civic Board society, there has been an attrition of the role of the Board as a policy maker and as a decision maker. This trend may be observed in some for-profit organizations as well. Hence, there needs to be a reassertion of the final responsibility for the Board not only to make decisions but, as we have repeatedly suggested, to make them of high quality.

Often, Board Members do find ways to avoid making decisions. Most frequently this is not something that they start out to do, but after a period of time they find out that they have, indeed, done it. The Decision Audit and Decision Autopsy procedures previously mentioned will help Civic Board Directors avoid decision slack—or cumulative inattention to actual decision-making functions. One should begin with the notion, however, that it is part of the responsibility of the Board Member to move the Board toward decisions.

Nondecision comes about in essentially two ways, which may operate separately but can also work interdependently. The growth of executive strength within the nonprofit organization is one reason why decisions get avoided by the Board; in fact, they may move into the executive cadre and be made there. Usually, very strong Executives who like this kind of style will "inform" Board Members of what was decided and seek their tacit approval. Large numbers of items on an agenda "for information" signal that some of this is going on.

On the other hand, ignorance about the kinds or levels of issues that should come up before the Board may limit decision making. Guidelines are an appropriate answer here. For example, some Boards will set dollar limits that require them to look at any expenditures that are above a certain amount. At other times, certain kinds of personnel actions are specified.

A second type of problem is attributable to the Board culture itself. Some Boards have a climate that is supportive of decision making. Other Boards are inclined to issue avoidance and minimization. It's not completely clear why the latter culture develops. Denial is something we all suffer from—no one likes to spend too much time working on things that are unpleasant. Sometimes an unfortunate press for consensus serves not to facilitate the progress of the group but, rather, to cause it to stall, sputter, and die.

Sometimes people actually believe they are making decisions, but the structure and nature of the procedures they use make it absolutely impossible for them to deal with issues effectively, efficiently, or even at all. This may be the most common situation. As we interviewed individuals and Boards that had serious difficulty in coming to grips with issues, they always had the feeling that they were, indeed, handling the issues. Volumes of material were presented to show how the Board had moved in one way or another. None of these movements, however, had been particularly effective. Furthermore, if we consider some of the larger corporations that have found themselves in serious trouble in the United States, the obvious question is, what were the Boards of Directors doing during the period of decline? It was not that they were doing nothing, but, in retrospect, that their strategic posture left something to be desired.

Civic Boards have an even more difficult time than the Boards of profit-making organizations in making the kinds of assessments that are required. The goals are squishier, the criteria are muggier, and, for people in the business community who are likely to serve on Civic Boards, the human service culture is somewhat foreign. It is harder, therefore, to develop the kind of crisp and clear assessments that everyone desires, and putting them into practice is somewhat problematic. Still, Members of Civic Boards should pay great attention to the responsibility of decision making. Trusteeship—the responsibility mentioned in the previous section—is something that focuses the attention of the Board on a range of issues and concerns. Decision making is what puts those concerns into some kind of useful package.

BOARD ORGANIZATION

One way to facilitate effective decision making is to develop the proper organization within the Board, itself, for it to happen. For most Civic Boards some kind of subcommittee structure is appropriate. First, however, something needs to be said about overall Board size and structure.

Very often the stationery of a Civic Board will list forty or fifty Board Members. Usually, such a situation comes about because the civic organization needs the implicit commitment of certain individuals' names. To this end, a tacit agreement is made with these individuals, permitting them the privilege of not coming to meetings too often or of not participating a lot. The problem is that such large Boards are not very effective. A smaller working group, or Executive group, in fact makes all the decisions. Therefore, a restructured working Board of about twenty-one or so individuals is probably the most useful solution. It is not necessary to lose the affiliation and implicit support of the others. If the individuals on the Board—those twenty-one we've just mentioned—were the "Directors," then it would be possible to have a larger group, or second tier, called "trustees," "friends of the organization," or something of that nature. This group could meet on a quarterly basis or twice a year, receive the annual report, and give advice on (or even vote on) the key elements of organizational governance and structure that the Board of Directors considers. It could also serve as a source of subcommittee Members for the Board of Directors. This arrangement can be used as a source of recruitment and training before Directorship is finally achieved. This sort of two-tier structure, or some variation of it, is worth considering in organizing the Board properly.

The problem with having larger numbers of individuals on Civic Boards seems to be that the thirty-, forty-, or fifty-Member Board is one where the individual Members do not take their responsibilities as seriously as they should—as Directors. They tend to view themselves more as general advisors to the organization and supporters of it. As a result, their commitment is limited, and this creates a problem.

There is also a tactical problem with respect to running these meetings. It's very difficult to tell who will turn up at the meetings, for example. Often, when the "occasional" Members do show up, they want to be provided with information on various issues, and they tend to be individuals who have not done their homework. This is a very difficult situation, for there is no assurance that those who show up will have a continuity of knowledge concerning issues. Thus, a smaller group, which takes Directorship as its responsibility—as distinct from the larger, less focused responsibility of trusteeship—is probably better than a Board of thirty or more.

Within this smaller Board, however, it is important that the group organize itself. Even a group of twenty-one that meets about once a month is not going to be the most efficient or effective decision-making body. Once there exists a poor and inefficient form for decision making, it is very likely that decisions will not get made. Subcommittees are important, therefore, because they enable a more detailed consideration of issues. Here, too, options and final recommendations are developed that can be brought to the full Board for final decision.

Typical subcommittees include the following: the Executive Committee, the Finance Committee, the Personnel Committee, the Program Committee. These may be what have historically been called "standing committees." They are at least typical if not always present. In addition there may be such committees as the Long Range Finance Committee, the Capital Improvements Committee, the Executive Search Committee, and the like. Generally, a Membership of about three is appropriate for each of the subcommittees. We like to draw the line at about five. Without keeping the subcommittee size down, it's very difficult to find times for subcommittees to meet. Indeed, an inordinate amount of energy can be spent simply finding meeting times and places.

Directors have to be aware of the importance and appropriateness of the subcommittee structure; for without it, it is unlikely that effective decisions will be made. What is more likely to occur is intensive and extensive discussion of issues lacking focus and purpose, leading to a range of nondecisions.

SELECTION AND EVALUATION OF THE EXECUTIVE

Of the key decisions made by Directors, few are more important than hiring the Executive Director and evaluating that individual. This is a problem that all organizations face.

The hiring process is really the end of a search process. The particular difficulty with looking for an Executive is that Boards don't do it often. There are a couple of general things to remember during the hiring.

It is most important actually to perform a search. Frequently, organizations will wait and, once a vacancy has been established, hope that appropriate individuals will apply. It's almost axiomatic, but it bears repeating here: some of the individuals the Board might like to have apply will not be those who will do so. Hence, Directors need to perform some outreach and identify individuals who they feel would be useful candidates. Having identified them, the Board should then ask them to consider discussing employment possibilities within the organization in question. (Asking them to apply is probably too big a step at this point.) This may be a sufficient way to interest some individuals.

It is also important to have some kind of written goal statement that can be shared with candidates for the position. Any prospective Executive would like to know the Board's goals. It should also be made clear to those who are being considered for the post, however, that the goal statement is open to some modification. Indeed, from an intellectual point of view, it is around the whole modification of organizational goals and directions that the greatest amount of discussion will occur. What might the potential candidate want to do, how far might he or she want to go, in what areas, and at what speed? All these questions deserve consideration.

It is frequently a good idea for Boards of Directors to place as little emphasis on the interview as possible. This suggestion may sound strange, but people who have been through the interview process know how bad a sample of behavior the interview can be. The interview can have two undesirable outcomes: the inappropriate rejection of a candidate who would have been excellent, and the inappropriate acceptance of a candidate who turns out to have severe limitations. We are not suggesting that an interview should not be held. Rather, a great deal of information should be garnered about the candidate before the interview occurs. In this way we can avoid putting too much weight where it does not belong. The truest indication of an individual's competence is his or her previous record of achievement. The Search Committee should spend most of its effort examining that record.

A lot of the difficulties surrounding the search are one-time problems for Boards of Directors (particularly because Boards tend to turn over every three years or so). The excitement of the search dies quickly, however, and the Executive fits in and goes to work. For a large number of Executives, that is the last they hear from the Board until they are fired or until they get some kind of awkwardly given raise! Civic Boards simply don't have well-accepted procedures for Executive evaluation.

It's very difficult to give a detailed discussion of the complex process of Executive evaluation here, but a couple of key points can be stressed. Most important may be the need to evaluate the Executive on the basis of a mutually agreed-upon set of yearly goals. But, as we mentioned, all too often evaluation does not occur.

A second problem develops when evaluation does occur—and then it is frequently after the fact. The Executive Committee will call in the Executive and give him or her a sense of how they think things have been going. The problem is that the Executive often hasn't known what the hopes and expectations of the Board really were. There is a way of overcoming this problem. We suggest that at the beginning of each fiscal year the Executive Committee ask the Executive to prepare a statement of hoped-for goals and achievements during the coming year. The Executive can include organizational goals, of course, but may list some personal development goals as well. These are reviewed by the Executive Committee and modified as they feel appropriate. The modified set becomes the working tool that the Executive uses to guide his or her effort during the coming year. Then, at the end of that year, the Executive is asked to prepare a report indicating how much achievement and accomplishment has been developed with respect to each goal. The Executive's report plus the assessment of the Executive Committee and whole Board in general become the basis for discussion with the Executive. This approach is rather simplistic, but it works reasonably well. Furthermore, it has the virtue of setting out in advance the kinds of hopes and expectations that the Executive should have.

TRAINING AND DEVELOPMENT

A final responsibility for the Board of Directors is its own training and development. This may seem surprising at first. Civic Boards have typically not viewed themselves as organizations or groups to be "trained" and "developed." We think this is an extremely unfortunate position and one that needs to be altered as quickly as possible.

In our complex society, with its increasingly complicated decision making, Civic Boards are going to need to assure their own competence as well as that of the Executive Staff. The common position that it is the Executive who needs to be trained and developed (as well as subalterns on the Executive Staff) now must be augmented to include the Board itself. If the Board is going to make good decisions, then it has the responsibility to look at its own decision-making mechanisms. Our rule of thumb is that a vigorous Board should provide for itself at least one training opportunity a year for each Member. Such a training opportunity can be a collective effort (a retreat or something of that kind), or it can be support for individual Board Members to attend meetings or conferences in the same way that staff do. Thus Boards will have to allocate some money from the budget for their own training. When budget time comes, this need should be seen to. Increasingly, work on Civic Boards should provide not only the aesthetic justifications of doing right and helping out, but should also be the occasion for learning and development on the part of individual Members. This is an important responsibility to meet.

CONCLUSION

In sum, the Civic Board is an important aspect of American society. It is the expression of the voluntary impulse, our habit of getting together to solve common problems. But, as it becomes an important part of the structure of society itself, we cannot leave it simply to good will and good intentions. Attention needs to be given to the ways in which decisions are made, Executives are hired, and structures are set up, to ensure that high-quality decisions are made.

PART V. COMMITTEEMANSHIP

The art of improving group decision making does not come easily to people. We outlined a variety of reasons for this at the beginning of this book. There are doubtless many more that could be given. As we talked with committee pros and meeting masters about what they do to make things go right, their skill was obvious. On the other hand, they weren't likely to formulate problems or concerns in an easily transmittable way. Rather, they tended to think in terms of episodes, vignettes, specifics. Chapter 16 touches on some of those specific and provides some guidance for applying the material presented in this book.

Chapter 17 focuses upon some suggestions for moving from the rather dismal current situation that afflicts many people to something more closely resembling what we've described herein. It's all very well to know what you *should* do, but getting there may be another matter altogether. We'll try to make it a little easier.

16
The Committee Meeting: A Brief Survivor's Manual

"I've wisdom from the East and from the West"
—W. S. Gilbert, *The Yeomen of the Guard*

This book has focused on effective decision making in meet-ings—how to achieve it, how to improve what you already have. We've talked about a number of specific types of attention that are required if the whole is to be improved. We have dissected the process that people experience and analyzed it for you, and have made some recommendations. But you may still feel isolated. In fact, we can imagine your saying something like, "Yeah, but they don't know the meetings I have. Everything's all jumbled up. It all comes at me in a mess, in a crush. Meetings are either death or booming, buzzing confusion."

Help—at least temporary help—is on the way. That's what this chapter is all about. Over the years we've worked with many different kinds of groups, helping them to improve both the meeting process and the quality of group-made decisions. One thing we've discovered is that there are strikingly similar prob-lems that tend to surface as we ask group Members to voice their most cherished hatreds in the meeting process. We're going to use some of them with you, and show you in each case how the problem can be addressed. Sometimes we'll be able to provide you complete solutions. You may adopt them, if you choose—

we know they work. For other kinds of problems we can only offer some guidelines, which at least should get you started toward achieving your own solutions.

The complaints usually fall into four broad groups: complaints about the Chair, complaints about the process within the meeting, complaints about some specific mechanical element, and that wonderful cluster of things known as "other." Even this division is subject to attack, however. A mechanical problem, such as inadequate room size, can immediately be taken as a deficiency of the Chair within the administrative role. A problem of process may well have some mechanical solutions and, hence, can be seen as a problem falling into the mechanics department—or it may be seen as a Member or Chair deficiency.

We're not going to spend a lot of time subdividing the problems into precise categories. Instead, we'll present you a few problem situations that seem to relate specifically to the Chair and a larger group that relate to Members. You may want to use these vignettes in your own staff meeting training situations. To that end, we've made a couple of simple training suggestions at the end of this chapter.

CHAIRS

Many problems focus on the role of the Chair and what responding individuals feel to be deficiencies within Chairship. So long as we remember that for every Chair problem there's a committee problem, we can begin looking at some of the difficulties.

Problem 1: *My Chair doesn't want to Chair. She has this fantasy that everyone's equal, and she never does anything. We're looking to her for leadership, and she keeps vacating the responsibility. How can we get her to take a more active role?*

Lack of training in the Chair role often creates problems like this. People erroneously believe that the Chair should not "run" the meeting. A number of designations have been developed to indicate Chairship like this; for example, "convener," "facil itator,'' ''mediator,'' and so on. There are certain types of meetings where those roles are appropriate. For decision-making groups, however, as the questioner suggests, somewhat more structure is appropriate.

Here are a couple of possibilities. Speak directly to the individual involved, using sections of this book or other appropriate references, and indicate that some additional structure would be appreciated, at least by some group Members. Alternatively, you or one of the other Members can propose that a meeting assessment be done. (It's usually good to clear this with the Chair first.) When the results are tallied, you can use them as the basis for discussion with the Chair.

Sometimes lack of Chair assertiveness is thought to be a personality characteristic. More often, however, we have found it to be simply a lack of knowledge about how to Chair, and how to convert and use techniques appropriate to other kinds of groups and settings in the Chairship role.

It's also possible for Members of the committee to take on some of the Chairship role collectively. In such a situation, one Member may say something like, ''I think we should move to closure on this,'' and others, hopefully, will agree. If the Chair is not acting in the particularly problematic way as a *tactic* to achieve certain objectives of her own, then there's likely to be no objection. This is *not* the best way to go, and should only be used in a sort of emergency situation.

Problem 2: *My Chair is too aggressive, always pushing, lashing, prodding us forward before we're ready. How can we skewer this guy?*

You have to look at the total picture here and find out exactly what's going on. This comment implies objections to ''speed'' and ''style.'' Ask yourself why the particular group isn't moving. Often, for a variety of historical reasons, groups hate to make decisions. Thus, any pushing in that direction is seen as obtrusive. Other times, of course, the Chair simply wants to move too fast. When that's the case, try announcing to the group, ''I think we are trying to move too fast. Why don't we try separating issues that require immediate attention and dealing with them, and hold back some others that we can give a little more time and thought to?''

Problem 3: *How do you handle a dumb Chair? This gal just doesn't seem to know which end is up. She must have been dumb to have accepted the Chair in the first place. Boy, she's really proving it now.*

Surprising as it may be, we hear this complaint rather frequently. It's a wastebasket type of complaint. There aren't any commonly agreed upon definitions of dumbness. Sometimes it means political naivete. Sometimes it means lack of intellectual prowess. Sometimes it means a penchant for foot-in-mouthism. As a catch-all, it's difficult to prescribe one specific solution. One thing that has worked in the past, however, is a training episode in which the entire group undergoes some training. Everyone benefits from the experience, so it's never a waste of time. With any luck, the Chair will benefit disproportionately more than others.

Problem 4: *Our Chair is just too weak. He flips and flops, does not talk directly or forcefully, is always tentative. Naturally, the group runs right over him. It's driving me crazy. I not only find it personally offensive, but our group doesn't get anything done.*

The case of the weak Chair is a classic case of projected Committee-itis. Obviously, there are individuals who take advantage of a Chair's competence problems. It's also obvious that other committee Members are not stepping in and dealing with that situation before it gets out of hand. The Chair selection process is one that often reaches out to inexperienced individuals. We make assumptions about their skills, only to discover, too late, that our assumptions are wrong. It is committee strength we're after here, though, not individual strength. Other Members of the committee should take advantage of the tentative openings proffered by the Chair and convert them into positive statements, thereby offering them to the committee for action. If the Chair says something like, "Well, I'm not sure if we should do A or B or possibly C; but then there's D and don't forget E and F . . . ," that's a golden opening. Say something like, "Based on our discussion, C seems like the way to go. Why don't we start with that?"

> Problem 5: *Our Chair is vicious and mean. He gets his way by attacking and intimidating individuals. It's not that he's pushy; he's vicious. He not only attacks the ideas people bring up, he attacks their integrity and motivation as well. Our group is now at a standstill.*

However tempting it might appear at times, the *least* preferred solution is to get the SOB alone in a dark alley and have the entire committee beat the living hell out of him. This is a case, however, where the individual should be contacted by committee Members immediately and outside of the committee room.

Attacking proposals of individuals is not a productive way to aid decision making. Unfortunately, too many individuals confuse vigorous debate *about* an idea with attack *of* the idea. On rare occasions when Chair dictatorship is a problem, we will record a committee session unobtrusively (even though we don't recommend the use of tape recorders as a general rule). Almost without exception, when Chairs hear the tapes, they are astounded and shocked by their own behavior.

If the facilities are available, it is often extremely useful to videotape a meeting. (If it's necessary, you can always claim it is for instructional purposes. Then, as you review the tape and discuss the experience with the Chair, the issue may emerge spontaneously.)

> Problem 6: *Our Chair is a damned monopolizer. She'll introduce the issue and then spend 20 minutes allegedly bringing us "up to date" on it. The way it seems to most of us now, this*

committee is merely a sinecure for the government. She tells us what's in the pipeline, what's going to happen or what has happened or what's going to happen 20 years from now. There's really no discussion, no other views are sought—none other, it seems would be regarded as relevant.

The monopolizing Chair is a phenomenon well-known to committee watchers. It can be handled in part through the establishment of subcommittees within the organization. Once that happens, a number of other individuals are necessarily involved. Often, poor structure within the committee leads to the Chair's undertaking many tasks and grumbling to others that the Members won't work. Subcommittee structures can often facilitate movement here.

Problem 7: *Our Chair doesn't know Robert's Rules of Order. Things are always a mess.*

Robert's *Rules* is not always useful. Prepared originally by a military man, it conveys a sense of items marching along in appropriate columns and with appropriate order. It may be helpful as one possible set of decision rules. You can also make up your own, and you might be advised to do so because the context varies from committee to committee. Any set of rules or conventions will do, such as those developed by the League of Women Voters, as long as they reflect good judgment and orderly process.

THE MEMBER

Problem 8: *We've got this one guy on our committee who never does a damned thing. If he volunteers for something, he'll usually start it, but someone else usually winds up finishing it. And if he gets assigned to something, you can just forget it. He usually won't even start if he hasn't volunteered.*

A number of problems focus loosely on the role of the Member. These usually happen because, for some reason, a Member is not carrying out an agreed-upon or assigned role.

Lack of follow-through is often the result of Members' very busy schedules. Sometimes it's the result of committee procedures teaching Members that there is no point in doing the work, since the likelihood of its being discussed or acted upon is extremely slim. Improve procedures and enforce the Rule of Agenda Integrity, and you will see a marked improvement. It may help for the Chair to follow through at the midpoint. Individuals may feel profoundly unable to do what they're asked to do, and they may need some help. The Chair can facilitate things here.

Problem 9: *We have one Member who is a revenge seeker and cannot accept any defeat, even the smallest one, graciously, and will fight tooth and nail for his point.*

There are several ways to skin this cat, but most of them involve ganging up with other committee Members. All too often individual Members feel great distress over a particular situation but won't talk to others about it, and don't see themselves collectively teaching the revenge seeker a lesson.

Such vindictive behavior tends to continue unless it reaches some kind of block; so it's imperative here that the Chair, in combination with the Members, call attention to it and, by pointing it out, create an atmosphere of negative reinforcement. You might try saying something like, "I don't think we want to engage in this kind of behavior."

Problem 10: *We have Members with no motivation. I really don't know why they're in the group at all. What can we do with them?*

Approach a nonmotivated Member privately and ask that very question. You might say something like, "Bill, I notice that you don't seem too interested. Is there some way that I or some of the others can make this a more meaningful experience for you?'' One of the things that Bill may reveal here is his dissatisfaction with procedures. His motivation may flag from constant rejection. If that's so, and he feels that a point of view he wants to offer hasn't been respected, then perhaps some changes can be effected.

Problem 11: *One of our Members is an agenda hider, always springing things on us, raising issues, causing chaos. It really is irritating.*

There are always problems with hidden agendas. This is a constant difficulty of committee life. It's also one of the difficulties that the Rule of Halves is designed to remedy. Too often when people are asked about hidden agendas, we hear the comment: ''Nobody ever asked me what I wanted to put on the agenda.'' There are, of course, Machiavellian characters who will deliberately lie or misrepresent their interests. We'll comment on them in just a moment. In the main, however, the straightforward approach of asking individuals for material soon enough for them to get the appropriate items solves much of the problem.

With respect to the Machiavellian creatures, an approach similar to the handling of the revenge seeker is appropriate: direct but diplomatic confrontation. Group pressure is extremely powerful. If it can be mobilized to stem the tide of influence of the hidden-agenda promoter, then success will be achieved.

Problem 12: *One of our Members is always offering to resign. We find that intimidating, and people don't know what to do. She'll say it forcefully and suggest that it's some big moral issue.*

This one is easy. The offer to resign should *always* be accepted. It represents an inappropriate domination of the committee process by a Member's interests. If a Member strongly wishes to resign, that is obviously the course that should be taken.

Problem 13: *How can we tell people things diplomatically? How can we avoid hurt feelings?*

It's not always possible to avoid hurt feelings. It's quite natural not to want to inflict pain on others, but when those others are, themselves, causing pain or disruption or are impeding the effectiveness of the group, then confrontation may be required. It's difficult to think specifically about diplomacy. A general rule we've found useful is that any reply that recognizes the contribution of a particular individual supports that individual in general but raises questions about a specific instance tends to be the kind of reply that is "diplomatic." Most of the time when we face an issue that requires "diplomacy," that's a signal that the issue might be better handled off the meeting floor than on it. People frequently become posturing and inflexible in public but are willing to talk in private. Sometimes humor can help as well. Consider the case above, accepting a resignation. Suppose you say, "I don't believe we should be forced either to accept Fred's resignation or to talk him into staying. In fact I feel that so strongly that if he does either, then *I'll* resign in protest." That ought to be enough to break the ice, and you can follow up by saying, "Seriously, I believe that we shouldn't permit ourselves to be put in these either–or boxes; we should explore other ways to solve the situation."

Problem 14: *We have several quiet Members. They never say anything. They just sit there. I don't even know why they come.*

Quiet Members need to be drawn out, and there are several ways to do this. First, under the Rule of Halves, ask them directly to contribute items to the agenda. Then, when those items come up, ask them to comment. Sometimes individuals or Chairs need to address people directly and ask them their view. At other times, a particular assignment requiring some report to the group is useful. It's been our experience that nonparticipants will respond well if the group shows a little initiative, indicating that their contribution is valued and welcomed.

> Problem 15: *We have an interesting problem in this committee. Sam is extremely well intentioned and well meaning, but a bumbler. He wants everybody to be happy. He's always worrying about this or that or the other thing. No matter what we come up with, he finds somebody whose interests have been trampled and becomes the champion of that interest. Sometimes things get pretty hairy. I think Sam really wants to help us out, but he is in fact our greatest hindrance.*

In the case of the well-meaning bumbler, a tightly organized agenda is a big help. The Chair and Members can use the agenda and indicate that the issue is now up for decision. Make it clear that there's only a certain amount of time available to deal with it. This strategy can shape the bumbler's behavior. Sometimes it helps to gently remind the group that some interests will lose under the proposed decision but that everyone's interests can't always be met.

People with these kinds of concerns are often "worriers"; that is, they worry a great deal about particular problems within the committee group but offer no suggestions or solutions. One useful technique is to hit them directly with a choice, something like, "Harry, I appreciate very much your point of view and I understand your concern. What I'd like to know now is, given the alternatives that we have, what is your recommendation? Where do you come down? I'd like to hear how you'd solve this particular problem." Another technique is to actually give the bumbler an opportunity to come up with a solution to a particular problem via a subcommittee assignment. Frequently, the worry and concern expressed for others masks a concern for self. Questions about why this or that interest was left out can on occasion be translated into "Why was I left out?" You can test such a hypothesis through a direct assignment.

Problem 16: *Several of our committee Members almost never show up. Then when they do come, they somehow expect us to start as if nothing had happened during the time when they weren't present.*

This is another case of committee compliance. It is admittedly difficult to confront Members with problems that accrue when they don't read minutes, don't check in, and then expect the group to pick up where they, rather than the group, left off. Confrontation may be necessary. However, the Chair or Member, if someone has been missing for a couple of meetings, can telephone and brief the individual, thus bringing him or her up to date in advance of the meeting.

More important, of course, is *why* they don't come. It's our experience that these are often the better rather than the poorer Members. They are the ones who have fuller schedules and simply aren't able to keep up with vacillating and changing committee times, poor procedures, and so on. Tightening up procedures may make their attendance more feasible.

Agenda and temporal integrity are important here. People are reluctant to come to meetings with uncertain starting and ending times. Most avoid the kinds of confrontations those irritations promote by staying away.

Problem 17: *We have a woman who always comes but doesn't do her homework. Then she asks a lot of detailed questions.*

The first question to ask is, was the material available in time? If it was, and if it is routinely available, then the question of agenda integrity comes up. Frequently people don't do homework because, as it turns out, it is extremely unlikely that the issue for which they did the homework will be discussed. If, however, we can be satisfied on both those counts, availability and scheduling of the material, then an out-of-committee approach to that individual and a sharing of problems that the behavior creates can be helpful. One member might be asked to comment individually in a meeting, saying something like,

"Sheila, we've had this for a week now, and I, as one Member, don't feel that I want to spend time reviewing it, unless there are a large number of people who had problems with it. [That's the left uppercut. Then, the helping hand:] But, perhaps what we can do is take a few minutes to summarize some of the key issues. That, I think, would benefit all of us."

> Problem 18: *There's a man on our committee who is simply an obstructionist. That's the only way I can describe him. No matter what is proposed, he's against it. I call him a "well poisoner." There are 100 reasons why everything anyone proposes should not, cannot, must not be done. At this point our group is reduced to absolute immobility.*

Here it is appropriate to confront the individual directly about his behavior. This can be done in the meeting or outside it. Generally, outside the meeting is best, and it's something that the Chair, as part of the Chair role, can undertake. This can be initiated by the Chair directly, or indirectly through the proposal of a meeting evaluation form, a committee assessment form, or an assessment of that type. Committee Members are typically unwilling to confront a person directly (as is required here), so more indirect methods might be appropriate initially. Such individuals, however, have from long experience become inured to such indirect methods. You might be forced to confront the individual directly in the meeting, saying something like, "Frank, you're a nay-sayer, and as I've listened to your remarks today, you've lacked positive comments on any of the proposals. This creates a negative climate. Maybe we could try to make both negative and positive observations.

Sometimes creating a role reversal situation helps. We've mentioned the Devil's Advocate Technique. Here's a man who is always a Devil's Advocate. In following this technique, he of course may spread his negativism to others. At the same time it's possible to develop an Angel's Advocate role, in which positive things are said. This positive role could be assigned to him fairly regularly, giving him the experience of playing a different, and opposite, role within the group.

Problem 19 (Women and Minutes): *As a woman, I deeply resent being asked to take minutes all the time. What should I do?*

Avoiding role stereotypes is always hard. It requires some degree of interpersonal or psychic cost. Often, the best way to handle such a situation is to make the implicit sexism more explicit: point out the stereotyping. If you want to deliver more of a message, however, passive aggression can be tried. Prepare a half page of minutes, clearly inadequate. Alternatively, or in concert with the other two techniques, accept with the proviso that you get to select the next minutes taker.

Problem 20: *Our committee is always referring to people in certain roles. For example, the Chair will ask the black Member of the committee what blacks think; women are asked what women think; and so on.*

Partly, the individual who is the unfortunate recipient of these kinds of remarks needs to take the lead. However, it's also possible for others distressed by it to cut in quickly, before the individual has had a chance to answer, and say something like, ''I think, in this committee at least, we should try to avoid treating people stereotypically. Mr. Jones can indeed comment on what the blacks think, if he wishes, because he is certainly capable of doing so; but I caution us all that that may not be a role he wants to play, and that may be a difficult role for him to extricate himself from. If we need this kind of information, or any other kind, let's make a more concerted effort to go out and talk to people ourselves.''

Whatever the issue, it's possible for the stereotyped individual to bring stereotyping behavior to the attention of the group. For its part, the group must also take that behavior into account.

Problem 21: *Our staff person talks a lot, participates a lot, and acts just like a Member of the committee.*

Staffer overparticipation often comes from a lack of understanding of the Staffer Role. In this case the Chair should have a discussion with the Staffer and try to convey what some of the problems are.

This problem is a difficult one because it is hard to be diplomatic. It's not just a case of talking too much, though that's part of it; it's overparticipation generally and an insensitivity to the appropriate level of participation. It's the "bad breath" problem of committee life: everyone's aware of it but reluctant to address it. Direct discussion by the Chair is, of course, one alternative. Passing along some material for the Staffer to read about his or her role is another. Both alternatives might be initiated through a meeting assessment form in which people anonymously indicate some of their concerns. This could be among them.

With that as a starting point, it's possible to take the next step.

Problem 22: *Recommendations come to our committee already signed, sealed, and delivered. We feel that a rubber stamp looks vibrant next to us.*

At least theoretically this problem has a relatively easy solution: move to the Options Memo format. Here, as in other areas, the phrase "easier said than done" takes on fresh meaning. Still, you can try to move in that direction by using the technique yourself. This lets you provide a role model for other Members. Alternatively, you can indicate that you've found a new technique and that you want to share it with the group as a discussion item. This is less personal than some of the other methods and, therefore, a little easier to initiate. A third possibility is to sit down with the Staffer and talk with that person about beginning to utilize Options Memos.

Problem 23: *The difficulty in our committee is that nothing ever gets done. We calmly sit, we talk and talk, but nothing ever happens.*

This kind of problem often stems from lack of clarity about committee purpose. You can solve it to a large extent by holding a meeting to review the purpose of the committee. It's astonishing in some cases how many other difficulties disappear once a crisper, more concise understanding is established. There may also be agreement on procedures. For example, after a certain period of time is given to discussion of an issue, a vote is taken. Individuals can be influential here. If you're in such a group, propose that the group begin to move ahead. Seek to play something of a catalyst role, even if you're not the Staffer. This is one place where initiative can be taken.

Problem 24: *Our group never starts on time, and it doesn't end on time either. It's so frustrating for all of us, especially those who come when the meeting is supposed to begin.*

Here again initiative can be taken by individual committee Members. Start by setting a personal policy for yourself: come when the meeting is supposed to begin; leave when it is supposed to end. This doesn't necessarily mean that you should be undiplomatic and blunt. Instead, try this approach: if the meeting is to end at three, say at the beginning, "I have scheduled another meeting for 3:10 so pretty much at 3:00 I'm going to have to excuse myself." This can be construed as modeling behavior for other committee Members, and it helps get the ball rolling. After a while, you can introduce this as an agenda item to the group itself, and indicate the need to consider the time. If it's appropriate to begin and end a bit later to accommodate schedules, that might be necessary. What's important is to have a published time, and then stick to it. Generally, there's an unwritten rule in groups that says if you haven't begun when people enter the room, they don't feel they are late. Therefore, no more than a

10-minute grace period (a sort of unwritten convention) is permitted. Then the meeting should begin. It should end exactly at the time indicated. If your personal policy says that it will end then, that's a step in the right direction.

> Problem 25: *Our group has no agenda. Everybody says they don't know what's going to come up until they get there.*

There are, of course, some groups in which lack of agenda is a plus, but they tend not to be decision-making groups. If a Member is faced with this kind of situation, a couple of options are open. One of them is, once again, to deal directly with the problem in the group itself. You might say something like, "I notice that we haven't had an agenda for these meetings; and it's very difficult for me, at least, to know what's coming up and to give it thought. I wonder if we couldn't agree to perhaps get one out that would come to us a couple of days before. I'd be willing to take some responsibility for checking with people and putting one together after conferring with the Chair, if that would be helpful."

A couple of points worth stressing are illustrated here. First is the sharing of your concern with the group. Second, and very important, is giving the group a specific action to take and offering to take that action. Often, when people share concerns with groups, they don't give the group an out. Then the group, as a group, is not sure what steps to take next. Providing the solution to a problem that has been raised gives the committee Member a chance to exert a greater degree of influence and cooperation. (Naturally, you would begin with the Rule of Halves, followed by the Rule of Three Quarters, in order to get the agenda out on time.)

> Problem 26: *We have staff meetings all the time. There's really no reason to follow the suggestions here. These aren't only my employees, they are my friends. I know these people. I know everything about them. And we manage to get things done in a pretty good fashion.*

In this actual case, the employees at the meeting didn't share their boss's sense of satisfaction. Many of them felt, in fact, that she was too controlling, too peremptory, and simply used the staff meetings as an oral newsletter. In point of fact, she didn't know very much about what people thought, and this was her mistake.

The fact that we know about people individually or collectively as friends and as colleagues doesn't mean that we know what they think on particular issues. We may believe that we know what they think, but often we can be surprised.

This case is a tough one because the Members, in organizational terms at least, are not status equals with the Chair/Boss. Any suggestion that may seem to have only minor committee or staff implications also has a number of implications for the person's relationships with the boss. Still, there are a few things you can try.

One of them is a direct discussion. Perhaps some of the material here could be shared with the boss. The division of items into information, decision, and discussion categories has often proved helpful. We would advise caution in the use of a meeting assessment form in staff meeting situations. Sometimes, if the boss finds even a residue of disaffection, it is difficult for her or him to move ahead. If the dissatisfaction can be left unstated, there may be more opportunity for progress. But, don't rule out the use of a meeting assessment form if no other strategy works to get the ball rolling.

Problem 27: *Our group seems to lack focus in its discussions. We wander here; we wander there; we get sidetracked. And, while we eventually decide something, it seems to have been a very circuitous process and not one that is very well organized or useful.*

The problems of agenda wandering and out-of-focus discussions often come as a result of the vagueness of the item on the agenda. Using the agenda format suggested in this volume, people know exactly what it is that they are discussing because there is a brief summary right below the item itself. This at least has the virtue of starting everyone off on the same footing. Typically, wandering behavior in groups, what is sometimes called a lack of germaneness in discussion, can't be handled because no one is sure what kinds of comments are in fact germane. Once that's been settled by a crisping-up of the agenda, the Chair can intervene and ask people to come back to the point. But Members can also do this. You might say something like, "George, I'm interested in your remarks, but I'm not completely sure how they relate to the item presently under discussion. Could you summarize your comments by telling me whether you're in favor of the proposal, against the proposal, or making a third proposal that we haven't heard yet?" Comments such as that, which needn't be made in a hostile or derogatory way, force George to fish or cut bait. While he might not want to do that yet, it at least sets the stage for anchoring his remarks.

Problem 28: *Our Members never seem to have time to come to meetings to do what needs to be done. They seem to rush in and rush out. The meeting is like a shooting gallery at the county fair, people coming in one door while other people are going out the other door.*

Don't think of this situation as a problem of time, and *don't* talk with individual Members about what is the best time to meet. Time is certainly a meeting problem but not in this case. All the situations we've run into such as this one tend to focus on lack of agenda integrity, lack of temporal integrity, lack of clarity and purpose. Like guests at a cocktail party, people drop into the gathering to be seen, to say a few words, and then get out. When we interview these Members, they tell us that they don't believe anything significant will be accomplished at the meeting; so, from their point of view, they are simply making a courtesy visit.

This problem can be remedied by vigorous attention to committee structure and process at the beginning of a series of steps that lead to committee productivity. Once Members realize that there *is* productivity, that something is actually going to happen, their flighty behavior tends to stop rather quickly.

Problem 29: *We can never find a time when everyone can meet.*

In this case time *is* the problem, and it's a very real one. The solution may require moving beyond the boundaries of acceptable times. Breakfast meetings and dinner meetings are, occasionally, worth trying. The problem actually stems in part from priority mixups. Establishing a vigorous group that orders its priorities and sticks to that order ensures that the battle is at least half won.

Problem 30: *We come into our committee room, and it's an absolute sty. The last group has left it a mess. We spend half our time cleaning up.*

This kind of problem is an irritant whose absence won't make a good meeting, but whose presence can ruin things. It's the job of the Chair or Staffer to come early and be sure that everything is in order. If need be, this role can be alternated weekly, but the goal is to have one individual arrive early to deal with any housekeeping tasks so that everything will be in order for the group. It's unreasonable to ask that the committee be both a decision-making company and a cleaning group. Not only is that irritating, but it also destroys the informal, cohesion-building, preliminary group time when people are coming in, chatting, sharing perspectives on particular issues, and so on. This is an important part of the group process and should not be destroyed. And, by all means, talk to the previous users of the room.

Problem 31: *Our reports are always passed out at the meeting. Sometimes it takes 15 or 20 minutes as page after page is given to us. I can't read them anyway sitting right there.*

Enforce the Rule of Three Quarters. Make sure stuff gets out ahead of time. This is usually a deadline problem, and report makers can work with a two-days-earlier deadline as well as they can with the deadline of the actual meeting time itself (in most instances). Report length may contribute to the problem. When it does, the Executive Summary Technique can be invoked, boiling down reports to a page or two that can be sent out. If by some chance there's a violation of the Rule of Three Quarters for some good reason, the Executive Summary Technique becomes even more important because most people have the ability to skim a page or two in a meeting if it is absolutely necessary.

Problem 32: *Our group doesn't seem to have the resource material available that we need when we discuss an item. There's a lot of generalized sharing of perspectives, but nobody ever really knows anything. And then the item often disappears and doesn't reappear for months and months.*

Part of the problem here stems from agenda ambiguity. It's sometimes useful to "noodle around" items, but then it must be made very clear to the Members that the discussion is a preliminary, and the sharing of perspectives is exactly what everyone is after.

On the other hand, if it's a decision item, then the group should agree not to go ahead unless there is adequate material available. One thing Members can do is make some advance phone calls. If the agenda comes out and requisite material is not enclosed, call and discuss the matter with the Chair. Usually, the Chair will be responsive to this gentle push and will, in turn, talk with those individuals who are getting the material ready and ask them to hurry. Sometimes you can get the Chair off the hook by saying, "I know you're busy; and, if it would help, I'll be happy to call Jim and Frannie and ask them to be sure and get the stuff ready on your behalf." Chairs usually leap at those kinds of suggestions.

CONCLUSION

Let's now do a little summarizing about some of the themes of these problems and these suggestions. First, the same problems appear repeatedly. There are, occasionally, unique problems in committee life and in decision-making group activity, but they're rare. By and large, problems of role performance, process, and mechanics come up again and again: "we don't get anything done," "the Chair doesn't chair," "we have dominating Members," "we can't find any time to meet." It's tiresomely repetitive, but it's also serious. If you don't shudder to think of the myriad of meetings that go on every day with these kinds of problems and difficulties, robbing us of our productivity and our quality, then you probably are wasting your time in meetings— and in reading this book.

What we have emphasized here is individual proactivity. Given that the things we have suggested provide a guideline for action, it's still very tough for you to try to be proactive, to try to express discontent when the solution to that discontent doesn't seem available either. Yet, in almost every instance, the problems that arise can be addressed by the rules and role suggestions we've given you. That should not surprise you. The rules were derived from interviewing committee pros. And, since the problems are common, their solutions have both commonality and applicability. Therefore, if you'll use these rules as a sort of handy-dandy guide, you can begin to take some initiative. You can intervene with concrete suggestions about what to do and how to do it.

The most useful thing to remember is that whenever anyone raises a problem in the group, offer to take the initiative in the search for a solution. You can use the normal group tendency to lay responsibility on the initiator to great advantage.

We've also talked about raising issues at the group level and using a meeting assessment form. We've provided a sample form at the end of this chapter. There are dozens of other types. Use this one, adapt another one, or use whatever seems appropriate. The assessment is more important than the form, so anything that permits individuals to express their views about how things have been going could be useful.

It's easy to construct a meeting assessment form. Simply convert each of the meeting rules into a question, or break them down into several questions. The Rule of Halves, for example, might look something like this: Do we get enough material, far enough in advance, for our meeting? You might convert the Rule of Three Quarters to something like: Does material get out in sufficient time for us to read and digest it? You could address the Rule of Temporal Integrity this way: How many minutes late are we in starting and ending our meetings? Solutions are available for the problems we encounter in meetings, but the problems must first be identified.

One thing we have not stressed in this discussion of individual problems is the matter of decision-group training and development. We did mention it when we talked about Civic Boards of Directors. You might want to refer to that chapter and apply those suggestions to decision-making groups generally. Most decision-making groups that meet on a regular basis should try to take some time each year for analysis and development. Call it a staff retreat or simply a training session, or anything you want. But take the opportunity to focus on ways to improve group decision making in a decision-making group. The time spent can pay enormous dividends.

Putting together such a training session isn't difficult. In almost every community of any size, there is at least one individual who is knowledgeable about group decision making and might be available to speak. Universities are veritable anthills of such expertise. There are also films on the subject that are both entertaining and instructive. Both XICOM Films in New York City and Time Life Films can provide films on how to run better meetings. Booklets and pamphlets can be distributed and discussed, and a facilitator can be appointed to lead the discussion or get it rolling. Once again, thoughtful attention to the process of decision making is really more important than the specifics, themselves.

We've found a couple of techniques especially useful for such training sessions, and you might want to try them. One is the "card technique"; the other is role playing in various forms.

In the card technique individual Members are asked to write down on separate 4 x 6 cards the most difficult problems they think exist in groups they are familiar with, including (or, if you wish, excluding) the current group. Those cards are then shuffled, and a facilitator asks individuals in the group to pick a card and read the incident described on it. After reading, the individual is asked to suggest a way of intervening. The problem statements in this chapter came from just such cards. The only rule is that one must reject his own card. This is an impersonal way to force some problems to surface in the group, by discussing how a situation might be improved without attaching a specific complaint to a specific individual.

With role playing, simply ask individuals to take over the role of Chair, Staffer, and so on. A version of the role-playing technique is pre-role-scripting, in which subgroups of individuals are asked to outline what the roles of Chair, Staffer, Member, and others would be. They then provide those scripts to other individuals in the group as the role play begins.

People in your group will have other suggestions about training episodes and techniques. Ask for them. Again, the important point is to spend some time self-consciously looking at the process rather than worrying abstractly about the proper styles and forms of training.

While the problems we have presented in this abbreviated survival manual do not cover every possible situation, they do demonstrate that for any problem that arises, there is a solution somewhere, requiring only the intelligent application of sound procedures that control the meeting and decision-making processes.

A SAMPLE MEETING ASSESSMENT FORM

1. What are the good things about this (committee) (group) (task force) meeting?

2. What are some of the bad things?

3. What are the aspects I would most like to see kept?

4. What are the aspects I would most like to see changed?

5. I would rate the meetings here (check one) A☐ B☐ C☐ D.

   (Explain the basis for your grade.)

17
How to Get from There to Here

"Climbing over rocky mountains . . ."
—W. S. Gilbert, *The Pirates of Penzance*

After all is said and done, what kind of steps or actions might you take to begin to move your staff meeting, interagency task force, board of directors, sales organization, or whatever, to a more effective and efficient meeting format? This is the process of group change, and it is a complex one, indeed. We've already taken the first step; we have a road map of where to go. One way to view the material we've presented is as an agenda for change. All too often groups have not worked out in their own minds what it is they want to do. Therefore, they become very busy over almost nothing. People call and say, "We would like to have a staff retreat. Can you help us?" The response is apt to be, "What are you retreating about?" There's a long pause; then an even longer pause. Finally, an answer comes: "Well, it just seemed like a good idea to get together and talk about things."

If even one or two individuals within a group have an idea of the direction change will take, then change is possible. Ultimately, the group itself will buy into the change; but, frequently, they'll play a wait-and-see game. Therefore, beginning with agenda preparation, there are some steps to take that will move the group toward acceptance.

Let's assume that you have read this book and find it persuasive and hopeful with respect to the decision-making groups you're involved in. Several courses of action are open to you. We'll get you started by outlining one direct, three-step approach and one indirect approach, based on the concept of "Propaganda-of-the-Deed."

A THREE-STEP DIRECT APPROACH

In a favorable, supportive environment, a direct approach is generally effective. Start by sitting down with your Chair/Boss and briefly reviewing the material presented here. Indicate the positive aspects of the situation, and offer to provide some leadership in developing a training program that would begin to implement some of these ideas. If the Boss agrees, then place a discussion item labeled "Improving Our Meetings" on the agenda. Copies of the material can be made available to the Members, and the process can begin.

If you happen to be the Boss, so much the better. Follow essentially the same route, but do so with a slight variation. It's usually a good idea to touch base in advance with a few individuals in the group, tell them that the subject of meeting improvement is going to come up, and ask them to skim the relevant material briefly in advance.

The "Improving Our Meetings" discussion is the first step in the three-step change strategy. This discussion is just a beginning during which people start to familiarize themselves with the material. This is a time for them to consider the idea that there may be new approaches, new techniques, whose use can lead to better meetings and higher-quality decisions. The goal of this discussion should be to agree to consider having a presentation of the material in a subsequent meeting. That presentation constitutes step two. Step three is a later special meeting, at which a proposal for a training session is specifically laid out. By that time Members will have had a chance to familiarize themselves further with the material, and will be in a position to talk more specifically about areas of emphasis.

It has been our experience that people relate more positively to relatively impersonal rules and relatively more personal roles.

While it is true that following rules and playing roles are things all people do, role training seems to be more ego-involving than rules. Thus the rules are usually an easier place to start. During the second meeting, individual input with respect to other topics to be covered, potential problems, and so on, is sought. Then, you, as the change agent, begin to plan a special third meeting at which the roles will be discussed.

This three-step process has often been a positive force for introducing new meeting mangagement techniques. There's an individual sense of discomfort/initiation that is seized upon by a particular individual—the change agent. With the support of the executive Boss, that individual begins the process of change. The three-step process is simply an initial phase, of course, in which group cooperation is enlisted and information provided.

AN INDIRECT, PROPAGANDA-OF-THE-DEED APPROACH

Let us suppose, however, that your Boss's reaction is either neutral or somewhat negative. In that case you'll require a more indirect process. You can begin by trying to introduce some of the techniques directly but subtly. Start by offering to prepare agendas or minutes. The strategy you will be employing is one in which the benefits of your system are recognized through their use. This indirect (or "Propaganda-of-the-Deed") strategy rests on the hope that once people begin to see that improvements are possible, they will request information about how and why this is happening and begin to seek to implement some of the techniques. You can think of it as a Show-and-Don't-Tell game.

It means that you will need to undertake more assignments and work in order to achieve your goal because it is important to get into Agenda Scheduler and Minutes Taker roles if the system is to be implemented. Both are crucial, fulcrum-type roles through which change can be leveraged.

TIMING

In both the direct case and the indirect case, change will take from six to nine months. It seems to take about that long for people to get used to a new system and to become comfortable in using it. Throughout that time there will be adjustments, changes, fall-backs, and diversions. Expect these as a normal part of the process. Change here, as anywhere, does not occur overnight. A number of people may need to be brought on board. In large corporations and organizations, for example, you may need to involve yourself in a whole network of meeting sites, committee groups, task forces, and so on. The time period may, in such cases, be even longer. However long it takes, you will have to develop an agenda for change based on the material suggested here. That will require mapping out the key centers and sites where information and training need to be applied.

Moving toward a new and improved organization of meeting activity should be viewed as a flexible and open process. The rules here should be grafted onto and into the organization's decision-making styles and modes. That may require some adjustment in our rules and our role definitions—which is quite all right.

How should you proceed after an initial phase of change has been accomplished? It's at this point that the meeting assessment form becomes an important tool. It *can* be used to initiate the process of change. The problem with using it this way is that disaffection and dislike of meeting processes tend to be so profound that respondents often become negativistic and sometimes hostile during the initial meeting evaluation session. No one's ever asked them how they like meetings; and, now that they have a chance to tell, they do so with a vengeance. Thus, if you're going to use a meeting assessment form as an initial intervention tool, it should be very brief and aimed at ways things can be improved rather than at what is wrong. Try to focus to as great an extent as possible on the positive.

Once the change process has been in effect for some period of time, ongoing assessments are important not only as a means of providing a way to spot glitches and problems but also to provide a way for people to share what are (we all hope) their positive feelings about the way things are going. This providing and receiving feedback serves to energize the change process even further.

CONCLUSION

There are many ways to begin a change process, and it is beyond the space available to us here to suggest all of them or even to deal with a few in great depth. We have, however, suggested a couple of ways to get you started in the process of moving toward better meetings. The three-step method suggested here is one direct strategy of change. The Propaganda-of-the-Deed strategy is an effective indirect method. In each case you will need to develop a plan of action and identify the sites requiring influence. You must then begin to move systematically in that direction. This may well be the most important point of all: to move systematically and thoughtfully toward meeting improvement. The techniques suggested in this book for improving group decision making will, in the final analysis, prove only a start—though a useful start—in achieving that goal.

PART VI. CONCLUSION

18
A Final Note

"Nothing could be more satisfactory."
—W. S. Gilbert, *The Mikado*

This book is about ways in which high-quality decisions can be made by decision-making groups. It may not be too much of an exaggeration to say that in contemporary American society there are hundreds of millions of committees, a veritable spider's web of committees, all involved in making some kinds of decisions minute by minute, hour by hour, day by day. How good these groups really are—how good the decisions they make are—is one of the vast uncharted territories of knowledge. We don't know a lot about them, but the process of charting and discovery is beginning.

We do know some ways in which these groups can be improved. This book is a small effort in that direction. The rules we have provided can be used as a generalized set of guidelines to assist committee managers and others in the development of more efficient and more effective committee process. The goal, of course, as we have stressed repeatedly, is not pleasant meetings—it is high-quality decisions.

Rules alone, though, are not enough. Individual roles have to be played out within the committee drama so that the rules can take effect. One must have a certain role repertoire, an ability to move from the role of Chair to the role of Member to the role of Staffer and back, sometimes within the same day or morning.

Each of us has this ability. Yet, because of ignorance about role requisites, we tend not to use it effectively and efficiently. We can only hope that the material we have presented here will help individuals, corporations, civic boards, and others to move to higher-quality decisions at lower cost.

Bibliography

Altman, Stan. "Performance Monitoring Systems for Public Managers." *Public Administration Review* (January/February 1979) 39, 1.

Anderson, John. "What's Blocking Upward Communication?" In *Current Perspectives for Managing Organizations,* Bernard M. Baas and Samuel D. Deep, (Eds.), Englewood Cliffs, N.J.: Prentice-Hall, 1970.

Argyris, Chris. "Individual Actualization in Complex Organizations." In *Organizations and Human Behavior: Focus on Schools,* Fred D. Carver and Thomas J. Sergiovanni (Eds.), New York: McGraw-Hill, 1969.

Argyris, Chris. *Reasoning, Learning and Action: Individual and Organizational.* San Francisco: Jossey-Bass, 1982.

Auger, B. Y. *How to Run More Effective Business Meetings.* New York: Grosset and Dunlap, 1964.

Baker, Robert (Ed.). *A Stress Analysis of A Strapless Evening Gown.* Englewood Cliffs, NJ: Prentice Hall, 1963.

Baruch, Hurd. "The Audit Committee, A Guide for Director." *Harvard Business Review* (May–June 1980).

Bennis, Warren G. "RX for Corporate Boards." *Technology Review* (December 1978/January 1979) 81, 3.

Bennis, Warren G. "The Crisis of Corporate Boards." *Technology Review* (November 1978) 81, 2.

Bernard, C. *The Functions of the Executive,* Cambridge, MA: Harvard University Press, 1968.

Berry, Waldron. "Beyond Strategic Planning." *Managerial Planning* (March/April 1981) 29, 5.

Bureaucrat X. *Cover Your Ass: or How to Survive in a Government Bureaucracy.* Edmonton: Hurtig Publishers, 1979.

Carroll, Daniel T. "Boards and Managements." *Harvard Business Review* (September–October 1981) 59, 5.

Cohen, Michael D. and James G. March. *Leadership and Ambiguity: The American College President.* New York: McGraw-Hill, 1974.

Cohen, Michael, James March and Johan P. Olsen. "A Garbage Can Model of Organizational Choice." *Administrative Science Quarterly* (March 1972) 17, 1.

Collins, B. and H. Guetzkow. *A Social Psychology of Group Processes for Decision Making*. New York: John Wiley and Sons, 1964.

Cox, Fred M. et al. (Eds.) *Tactics and Techniques of Community Practice*. Itasca: F. E. Peacock, 1984.

Cox, Fred M. et al. (Eds.) *Strategies of Community Organization*. 3rd Edition. Itasca: F. E. Peacock, 1979.

Daft, Richard L. and Patricia J. Bradshaw. "The Process of Horizontal Differentiation: Two Models." *Administrative Science Quarterly* (September 1980) 25, 3.

Dale, Ernest. *Management: Theory and Practice*. 3rd Ed. New York: McGraw-Hill, 1973.

Dearborn, DeWitt and Herbert Simon. "Selective Perception: A Note on the Departmental Identifications of Executives." *Sociometry* (1958), 21, 2.

Doyle, Michael and David Strauss. *How to Make Meetings Work*. New York: Wyden Books, 1976.

Drucker, Peter F. *The Practice of Management*. New York: Harper and Brothers Publishers, 1954.

Drucker, Peter F. "Managing the Public Service Institution." *Public Interest* (Fall 1973), No. 33.

Drucker, Peter F. *Management: Tasks, Responsibilities, Practices*. New York: Harper & Row, 1974.

Drucker, Peter F. "Deadly Sins in Public Administration." *Public Administration Review* (March/April 1980) 40, 2.

Dunsing, Richard J. *You and I Have Simply Got to Stop Meeting This Way*. New York: American Management Association–Amacom, 1978.

Fenn, Dan H, Jr. "Executives as Community Volunteers." *Harvard Business Review* (March/April 1971) 49, 2.

Fiedler, F. E. et al. "Organizational Stress and the Use and Misuse of Managerial Intelligence and Experience." Bibl., *Journal of Applied Psychology* (December 1979) 64, 6.

Filho, Paulo De Vasconcellos. "Strategic Planning: A New Approach." *Managerial Planning* (March/April 1982) 30, 5.

Ford, Charles H. "MBO; An Idea Whose Time Has Gone?" *Business Horizons* (December 1979) 22, 6.

Ford, Charles H. "Management By Decisions, Not by Objectives." *Business Horizons* (February 1980) 23, 1.

Forester, J. "Critical Theory and Planning Practice." Bibl., *American Planning Association Journal* (July 1980) 46, 3.

Fowler, Phyllis Ann. The Committee as an Interacting Small Group." Dissertation, Wayne State University, 1972.

Frohman, Alan L. and Steven P. Ober. "How to Analyze and Deal with the Basic Issues." *Management Review* (April 1980) 69, 4.

Giermak, Edwin A. "Individualism vs. the Committee Process." *Advanced Management* (December 1960) 25, 12.

Glass, Joseph G. *How to Plan Meetings and Be a Successful Chairman.* New York: Merlin Press, 1951.

Goffman Erving. *The Presentation of Self in Everyday Life.* New York: Anchor, 1959.

Greenleaf, Robert K. *The Servant as Leader.* Cambridge, Mass: Center for Applied Studies, 1970, 1973.

Greenleaf, Robert K. *The Institution as Servant.* Cambridge, Mass: Center for Applied Studies, 1972, 1976.

Greenleaf, Robert K. *Trustees as Servants.* Cambridge, Mass: Center for Applied Studies, 1974, 1975.

Greenleaf, Robert K. *Servant—Retrospect and Prospect.* Cambridge, Mass: Center for Applied Studies, 1980.

Griffiths, Daniel E. "Administration as Decision-Making." In *Organizations and Human Behavior: Focus on Schools,* Fred D. Carver and Thomas J. Sergiovanni (Eds.), New York: McGraw-Hill, 1969.

Groobey, John A. "Making the Board of Directors More Effective." *California Management Review* (Spring 1974), 16 3.

Gummer, Burton. "A Framework for Curriculum Planning in Social Welfare Administration." *Administration in Social Work* (Winter 1979), 3, 4.

Haft, Robert. "Business Decisions by the New Board: Behavioral Science and Corporate Law." *Michigan Law Review* (November 1981) 80, 1.

Haga, W. J. "Managerial Professionalism and the Use of Organization Resources." *American Journal of Economics and Sociology* (October 1976) 35, 4.

Hall, Jay. "Decisions, Decisions, Decisions." *Psychology Today* (November 1971), 5, 6.

Hamby, Russel. "Gender and Sex-Role Behavior in Problem Solving Groups." *Sociological Focus* (August 1978), 11, 3.

Handbook for Legislative Committees. The Council of State Governments, 1313 East 60th Street, Chicago, IL 60637 (January 1963).

Harari, Ehud. "Japanese Politics of Advice in Comparative Perspective." *Public Policy* (Fall 1974) 22, 4.

Herbert, W. R. "Effective Time Management." *Public Management* (January 1979) 61, 1.

Holloman, Charles R. and Hal W. Hendrick. "Adequacy of Group Decisions as a Function of the Decision Making Process." *Academy of Management Journal* (June 1972) 15, 2.

Houle, Cyril Orvin. *The Effective Board.* New York: Association Press, 1960.

Huseman, Richard C. et al. "Planning for Organizational Change: The Role of Communication," *Managerial Planning* (May/June 1980) 28, 6.

Ingalls, John D. *A Trainer's Guide to Androgyny.* Rev. Ed. Washington, D.C.: U.S. Department of Health, Education and Welfare, 1973.

Janis, Irving L., "Groupthink." *Psychology Today* (November 1971) 5, 6.

Janis, Irving L., and Leon Mann. *Decision Making*. New York: The Free Press, 1977.

Jay, A. "How to Run a Meeting." In *Tactics and Techniques of Community Practice*, F. Cox et al. (Eds.), Itasca: F. E. Peacock, 1977.

Jones, C. "If I Knew Then . . ." (A Personal Essay on Committees and Public Policy)." *Policy Analysis* (Fall 1979) 5, 4.

Juran, J. M. and J. Keith Louden. *The Corporate Director*. New York: American Management Association, 1966.

Kantor, R. *Men and Women of the Corporation*. New York: Basic Books, 1977.

Kaufman, Debra and Michael Fetter. "Work Motivation and Job Values among Professional Men and Women: A New Accounting." *Journal of Vocational Behavior* (December 1980) 17, 3.

Kent, Glenn H. "Team Management of Pension Money." *Harvard Business Review* (May–June 1979) 57, 3.

Kernbert, O. F. "Regression in Organizational Leadership." *Psychiatry* (February 1979) 42, 1.

Klein, Harold E. and William H. Newman. "How to Integrate New Environmental Forces into Strategic Planning." *Management Review* (July 1980) 69, 7.

Klopfer, Frederick J. "Decision Rules and Decision Consequences in Group Decision Making." Unpublished Doctoral Thesis, Texas Tech University, 1975.

Levinson, Daniel and Gerald L. Klerman. "The Clinical-Executive." *Psychiatry* (1967) 30, 1.

Levy, Leslie. "Reforming Board Reform." *Harvard Business Review* (January–February 1981) 59, 1.

Likert, Rensis and Jane Gibson Likert "A Method for Coping with Conflict in Problem Solving Groups." *Group and Organizational Studies* (December 1978), 3, 4

Lindblom, C. E. "The Science of Muddling Through." *Public Administration Review* (Spring 1959) 19, 2.

Machlowitz, Marilyn. *Workaholics*. Reading, Mass: Addison-Wesley 1980.

Maier, Norman R. F. *Problem Solving and Creativity in Individuals and Groups*. Belmont, CA: Brooks/Cole, 1970.

March, James G. and Herbert A. Simon. *Organizations*. New York: John Wiley and Sons, 1958.

Mazzolini, Renato. "How Strategic Decisions Are Made." *Long Range Planning* (1981) 14, 3.

Messeha, Refaat Fayek. *"A Critical Analysis of the Board of Directors: Selection, Election, Structure, Performance, and Compensation."* Dissertation, The University of Wisconsin, 1966.

Michael, Stephen R. "Feedforward Versus Feedback Controls in Planning." *Managerial Planning* (November/December 1980) 29, 4.

Mileti, Dennis et al. "Structure and Decision Making in Corporate Organizations." Bibl., *Sociology and Social Research* (July 1979) 63, 4.

Moore, Joan W. "Patterns of Women's Participation in Voluntary Associations." *American Journal of Sociology* (May 1961) 16, 6.

Moore, Mark H. "Policy Managers Need Policy Analysis." *Journal of Policy Analysis and Management* (Spring 1982) 1, 3.

Morris, Seymour, Jr. "Managing Corporate External Affairs." *Management Review* (March 1980) 69, 3.

Muller, Robert Kirk. *Board Life: Realities of Being a Corporate Director.* New York: AMACON, 1974.

Naisbett, John. *Megatrends.* New York: Warner Books, 1982.

National Information Bureau. *The Volunteer Board Member in Philanthropy.* New York: National Information Bureau, 1979.

Naylor, Thomas H. "How to Integrate Strategic Planning into your Management Process." *Long Range Planning* (1981) 14, 5.

Naylor, Thomas H. and Kristin N. Neva "Design of a Strategic Planning Process." *Managerial Planning* (January/February 1980) 28, 4.

North, Joan. "Guidelines and Strategies for Conducting Meetings." *POD Quarterly* (September 1980), Vol. 2, 2.

Ouchi, William. *Theory Z.* Reading, Mass: Addison-Wesley, 1981

Parsons, Talcott. "Suggestions for a Sociological Approach to the Theory of Organizations." In *Complex Organizations: A Sociological Reader,* Amitai Etzioni (Ed.), New York: Holt, Rinehart and Winston, 1961.

Pascale, R. T. and A. Athos. *The Art of Japanese Management.* New York: Simon & Schuster 1981.

Perham, John C. "Non-Profit Boards under Fire." *Dun's Review* (October 1979) 14, 4.

Peter, Laurence J. *The Peter Prescription.* New York: William Morrow, 1972.

Peter, Laurence J. and Raymond Hull. *The Peter Principle.* New York: William Morrow and Company, 1969.

Pogrebin, Letty Cottin. *How to Make It in a Man's World.* Garden City, NY: Doubleday, 1970.

Prince, George M. "How to Be a Better Meeting Chairman." *Harvard Business Review* (January/February 1969) 47, 1

Quick, Thomas L. "The Many Uses of a Task Force." *Personnel* (January 1974) 51, 1

Ridel, J. A. "Citizen Participation: Myths and Realities." *Public Administration Review* (May/June 1972) 32, 3.

Rittel, Horst W. J. and Melvin M. Webber. "Dilemmas in a General Theory of Planning." *Policy Sciences* (June 1973) 4, 2.

Roberts, General Henry M. *Roberts Rules of Order,* New and Revised Edition by Sarah Corbin Roberts. New York: Scott Foresman, 1970.

Ross, Aileen, D. "Control and Leadership in Women's Groups: An Analysis of Philanthropic Money-Raising Activity." *Social Forces* (December 1958), Vol. 37, No. 2.

Ross, Aileen D. "Philanthropic Activity and the Business Career." In *Social Welfare Institutions,* Mayer Zald (Ed.), New York: John Wiley, 1965.

"Run A Meeting That Gets Things Done." *Changing Times* (September 1969) 23.

Schmidt, Richard. *"The Relationship between Inside-Outside Representation on Boards of Directors and Selected Measures of Economic Performance, Financial Structure, and Business Policy."* Dissertation, New York University, Graduate School of Business Administration, 1974.

Schwartz, Felice N. "Invisible Resource." *Harvard Business Review* (March–April 1980) 58, 2.

Selznick, Phillip. *Leadership in Administration.* New York: Harper and Row, 1957.

Seward, Jack. *The Japanese.* New York: William Morrow, 1972.

Simon, Herbert. *The New Science of Management Decision.* New York: Harper & Brothers, 1960.

Singer G. and M. Wallace. *The Administrative Waltz or Ten Commandments for the Administrator.* Oxford: Pergamon Press, 1976.

Stern, Alfred R. "Instilling Activism in Trustees:" *Harvard Business Review* (January–February 1980) 58, 1.

Strauss, Bert and Frances. *New Ways to Better Meetings.* Revised Edition. New York: Viking Press, 1964.

The Conference Board. *The Board of Directors: New Challenges, New Directions.* New York: The Conference Board, 1972.

Tillman, R., Jr. "Problems in Review: Committees on Trial." *Harvard Business Review* (1960), 38, 3.

Tropman, John E. "A Comparative Analysis of Community Organization Agencies." In *Community Organization: Studies in Constraint.* I. Spergel, Beverly Hills: Sage Publications, 1972.

Tropman, John E. "The Effective Committee Chair: A Primer" *Directors and Boards* (Summer 1980).

Tropman, John E. *The Board of Directors.* Vermont: Youth Services Institute, 1981.

Tropman, John E., Harold R. Johnson and Elmer J. Tropman. *The Essentials of Committee Management.* Chicago: Nelson-Hall, 1979.

Vogel, Ezra. *Japan as Number One: Lessons for America.* Cambridge, MA: Harvard University Press, 1980.

Vroom, Victor H. and Philip W. Yetton. *Leadership and Decision-Making.* Pittsburgh: University of Pittsburgh Press, 1973.

Wills, Garry. *The Kennedy Imprisonment*. Boston: Little, Brown and Company 1982.

Yarborough, Joanne. *Women in Management: Selected Recent References.* Washington, D.C.: U.S. Dept. of Labor Library, U.S. Government Printing Office, 1978.

Zander, Alvin. *Making Groups Effective,* San Francisco: Jossey-Bass, 1982.

Zelman, W. "Liability for Social Agency Boards." *Social Work* (July 1977), 22 (4).

Ziller, Robert C. "Four Techniques of Group Decision Making under Uncertainty." *Journal of Applied Psychology* (December 1957), 41, 6.

Index